Caribbean Primary Mathematics

Level 3 Teacher's Guide

Contents

Introduction — 3

    Using the *Caribbean Primary Mathematics* series — 3

    Lesson planning — 4

    Assessment — 5

    Integration — 6

    Technology — 6

    Problem solving — 6

    Realistic and practical activities — 7

Teaching and learning materials — 8

    The importance of teaching and learning materials — 8

    Types of materials — 9

    Resources in and around your classroom — 10

    Building up a collection of materials — 11

    Using materials in the mathematics classroom — 13

    Using selected materials — 15

    References and further reading — 18

Unit-by-unit support — 19

Level 3 curriculum coverage grid — 85

Introduction

Using the *Caribbean Primary Mathematics* series

The *Caribbean Primary Mathematics* series was originally developed and tested by members of the UWI School of Education and schools. This edition has been revised by a pan-Caribbean team of educational experts, with the following features.

Meeting the latest curriculum objectives
We have updated the tried and tested course to meet the requirements of the latest curricula in each of the Caribbean territories. In each Teacher's Guide, you will find a grid that outlines how the curriculum objectives are covered in the course for that level. In some cases, a concept may not be required by the curricula of all the territories. You will find notes in the suggested approach for each chapter, pointing out which activities to leave out if they are not relevant to your students.

Up-to-date curriculum objectives
In Levels 1, 2 and 3, the series follows a spiral approach to learning. Spiralling means that every new concept is reinforced at calculated levels and extended as time goes on. Materials are organised into discrete, manageable units linked to curriculum topics.

Relevant contexts for learning
Throughout each level, you will find 'talk about' boxes, illustrated with the CPM parrot, which provide topics for class discussions around topical issues relevant to the material covered on that page.

Interactive CD-Rom activities
In this new edition of *Caribbean Primary Mathematics*, each level comes with a CD-Rom packed with interactive activities for students to consolidate their learning of the key topics. There are references throughout the Teacher's Guide indicating when these activities are to be played. These are marked with the symbol.

Practical activities
Wherever you see the symbol in the Pupil Book, students have an opportunity to explore or investigate a mathematical concept through a practical, hands-on activity. If you need any resources for these activities, they will be listed under materials at the beginning of the suggested approach for that unit.

Classroom testing and additional activities
In the Pupil's Book, assessment material is provided at regular intervals. In the Level 3 Teacher's Guide, we provide additional ideas for assessment, giving you the opportunity to assess your students' progress and identify areas that require more practice. We also provide additional activities in the suggested approach for each unit.

Approaches to computation

You need to make the students aware that some situations require the use of calculators, while others require a combination of mental or pencil-and-paper working. Students need to learn when to use the most appropriate strategy in a given situation.

When students come across a problem that they cannot easily work out mentally, they should get into the habit of first estimating the answer. This will help them to know whether they have carried out the calculation correctly or not. Students should also check the reasonableness of their answers. This is especially important in word problems. Students should look back at the question and decide whether they have answered the question that was being asked, and whether their answer makes sense in the context of the problem.

Lesson planning

It is important for you to plan your lessons before entering the classroom. Whether the plan is very detailed or only a brief outline of activities, it helps you to keep a record of what is to be taught. A lesson plan describes what is to be done, when it is to be done, how long it should take and what resources are needed.

One form of the lesson plan that is used widely in mathematics is known as the *Hunter Lesson Cycle*, so named because of the way the sequence of events may be repeated. The components of the Hunter Lesson Cycle are:
1 Set the stage
2 State the objective
3 Provide instructional input
4 Model operations
5 Check for understanding
6 Give guided practice
7 Give independent practice.
8 Assess mastery

You may want to follow the Hunter Lesson Cycle, or you could use a more informal plan. Any lesson plan has three main components: the beginning, the middle and the end.

Assess readiness

↓

Set the stage
- Motivate

↓

State the objective
- Relate to prior knowledge

→

Provide instructional input
- Label concepts
- Define terms and symbols

↓

Check for understanding
- Ask questions
- Observe operations
- Reteach, if necessary

←

Model operations

↓

Give guided practice
- Students demonstrate skills
- Students extend concepts
- Students work examples
- Students repeat operations

↓

Give independent practice
- Students practise skills

↓

Assess mastery
- Ask questions
- Observe students
- Give tests

Beginning
- Set out the purpose of the lesson.
- Make connections to previous lessons or material covered.
- Initiate a participatory activity which stimulates the students' interest.

Middle
- Introduce the mathematical concepts.
- Demonstrate some examples of what the students are expected to do.
- Give students time to complete their activities and tasks.
- Assess and evaluate the students' work.

End
- Summarise the lesson and learning activities, orally or through an activity
- Indicate what the follow-up to the lesson will be.

Assessment

Traditionally, assessment has comprised mainly written tests. While these are important in determining the progress of students, especially when a grade or mark is required, there are other forms of assessment that should be included in the mathematics classroom:
- questions and tasks
- practical investigations and activities
- homework
- group work
- self assessment.

Questions and tasks
Remember, you cannot assess all students at the same time. During any lesson, ask questions and set tasks that allow you to assess some of the students. Gradually, you will build up a clear idea of each student's progress. Make sure that the questions are clear and that students know what they are expected to do.

Practical investigations and activities
Most practical activities require pair or group work. The students will often have to share their answers with the rest of the class. This provides an opportunity for you to assess problem-solving and presentation skills.

Group work
Group work gives you an opportunity to assess each student's social skills and communication skills. More confident students will often dominate the group; make sure that you ask questions aimed at the more reserved members of the group in order to assess their contributions too.

Self-assessment
In many cases, you can ask students to check each other's work or their own work. It is also important to ask students which parts of the lesson they found easiest or most difficult, as they often have a clear idea of the areas in which they want more practice.

Integration

Integration should be included in all aspects of mathematics instruction, both within mathematics and across mathematics and other subject areas. Firstly, within mathematics, a topic such as money cannot be introduced or reviewed without reference to related topics such as decimals, operations on numbers or place value. Secondly, many topics in mathematics are common to topics in other subject areas: measurement in science, shapes in art, and map locations in social studies can all be reinforced in the mathematics classroom. Integration provides opportunities for the subject teachers to plan more effective lessons, in collaboration with other subject teachers. This helps the students to recognise that mathematics is not an isolated subject, but a component of all other subjects.

Technology

Technology can form an integral part of all mathematics instruction, used by both the teacher and the student. Technology may include computers, overhead projectors, television, tape recorders, CD players and, of course, calculators. Computers provide immediate access to world-wide resources, visual stimuli and simulations of otherwise remote activities, and contact with students in other places. In addition to these benefits, there are many other advantages to using technology in schools. Technology enhances the student's motivation in many ways. Students see technology as something fun and exciting. It immediately grabs their attention. Technology also enhances creativity as students have the opportunity to create their own materials. Each student can determine the pace at which to proceed and thus gains more control over the learning that takes place. Technology helps the teacher to produce resources and assignments, to execute varied and interesting lessons and to store these materials efficiently over long periods. Technology is therefore an asset for both the teacher and the student.

Problem solving

Although problem solving is an integral part of mathematics instruction, many teachers teach problem solving as a separate concept. Instead, problem solving should be incorporated at all stages of the instructional process – when introducing a concept, throughout the instruction and as part of the assessment. Problem solving provides an opportunity for students to communicate, reason, explore and investigate in the mathematics classroom, thus encouraging a better understanding of the concepts.

There are four general stages involved in finding the solution to a problem. These are:
- understand the problem
- devise a plan
- carry out the plan
- check the solution.

There are many problem-solving strategies that may be used, depending on the problem to be solved. These include:
- draw a diagram
- guess and check/trial and error
- solve a simpler problem
- act out the problem

- make a model
- look for a pattern.

Realistic and practical activities

Mathematics must be taught in such a way that the students enjoy what they are doing and relate it to their everyday lives. Along with the activities suggested in the *Caribbean Primary Mathematics* series, you should include activities that are realistic and practical. In addition, students must recognise the link between mathematics and their daily lives and experiences. We all use mathematics on a daily basis: we tell the time, we measure amounts when we serve and eat food, we estimate whether clothing will fit, we read maps ... just to name a few daily mathematical processes. Carpenters, painters, accountants and doctors are some of the people who depend on daily use of mathematics. For children, activities such as running races, skipping or playing card games all involve some mathematical understanding. These types of activities are ideal for teaching mathematics to ensure that all children, especially those who struggle with mathematics, become more confident and competent in their mathematical abilities.

Teaching and learning materials

Learning aids enable students to develop their mathematical knowledge and competencies. Student books and textbooks are examples of everyday learning aids. However, in order for students to gain real understanding of mathematics, they need to encounter a range of teaching and learning materials that give them practical experience in using mathematical concepts. This section tells you about the range of materials that you can use in your classroom. We offer suggestions about obtaining and using mathematics materials, and provide detailed information about:
- the importance of mathematical materials
- types of materials
- how to build up a collection of materials
- how to use different types of materials in your classroom
- activities related to specific materials.

The importance of teaching and learning materials

Teaching and learning materials are important because:
- they engage the students in practical, hands-on learning
- they offer concrete examples and applications of mathematical concepts, skills and procedures
- they stimulate interest, perseverance and problem-solving skills.

Each of these points is discussed in more detail below.

Combining hands-on activity with mental activity

Students learn best by doing things, by being actively engaged in the teaching/learning process. Active engagement may involve physical activity, but it should always require some form of mental activity (Anthony, 1996). For example, students may examine or use selected objects. While doing this, the students should also be required to engage in mental activities such as justifying, discussing, comparing and contrasting mathematical ideas. Learning materials facilitate practical activities, which also engage students mentally.

Progressing from the concrete to the abstract

Students at the primary level are seldom able to do mathematics solely at the symbolic or abstract level. Teaching and learning materials enable students to examine specific examples of concepts, skills and procedures, and to generalise from these examples. The materials also allow students to link the mathematical concepts to their experiences and to previous learning. Thus, teaching and learning materials can help students to learn mathematics meaningfully.

Stimulating students' interest and perseverance

Well-prepared, appropriate materials capture the students' attention, motivating them to engage with the mathematical learning process and stimulating their interest in mathematical tasks. In this way, teaching and learning materials develop students' problem-solving skills. Personal qualities – such as perseverance and willingness to engage in tasks – facilitate mathematical learning, but these qualities are also improved through the use of mathematical learning and teaching materials.

Types of materials

You can use a wide range of materials in your classroom, including found objects and materials, second-hand items and bought products. In this section we categorise materials in two different ways:
- according to the stages of mathematical development supported by each material
- according to the form of the material.

There are many other ways of categorising materials, but this section aims to give you a broad idea of the variety of materials available.

Supporting mathematical development through materials

In this course, we recommend that students begin with concrete examples and gradually move towards working with abstract concepts. Grossnickle, Reckzeh, Perry and Ganoe (1983) divide materials into three groups which are linked with this progression from concrete to abstract.

- **Manipulatives** are objects that the students can feel, touch, handle and move. Examples include dice, cards, paper, clay, string, and so on. These materials are linked to mathematical development through concrete examples.

- **Visual, audio and audio-visual materials** require students to use their senses of sight and hearing. Visual materials involve looking or watching. Examples include pictures, diagrams and photographs. Audio materials involve hearing or listening. Examples include CDs, cassette tapes, rhymes and songs. Audio-visual materials involve a combination of watching and listening. Examples include films, videos and some computer software. These materials are linked to a semi-concrete stage of mathematical development.

- **Symbolic materials** represent mathematics through words, numbers and symbols. Examples include textbooks, pupil books, worksheets and other texts. Symbolic materials are linked to the abstract stage of mathematical development.

In order to progress from the concrete to the abstract when teaching each mathematical skill or concept, you would usually introduce the work using manipulatives. You could then gradually move towards the semi-concrete stage using audio-visual materials, and finally progress towards the abstract stage using symbolic materials.

Different forms of materials

We can also categorise materials according to form. Materials take four different forms: manipulatives, print materials, games and puzzles, and technological devices. The table below outlines these forms and gives some examples of each. Remember, these categories are not mutually exclusive. For example, software packages could include games and puzzles as well as print media. However, this table is intended to give you an idea of the sheer range of materials available.

Type of material	Description	Examples
Manipulatives	Materials that students can handle, feel, touch and move	■ Real-life objects such as shells, seeds, buttons, money ■ Objects specifically designed to represent mathematical ideas, e.g. geo-boards, abaci, base ten blocks, geometrical shapes or models
Print materials	Materials that convey information in words, pictures or diagrams	■ Activity cards that outline tasks ■ Student books and worksheets ■ Flash cards ■ Charts
Games and puzzles	Games are activities that are guided by rules; puzzles are non-routine problems	■ Commercial games, e.g. snakes and ladders, dominoes, card games ■ Teacher- or student-made puzzles and games
Technological devices	Materials that require electronic or other technology	■ Calculators, films, videos, audio cassettes/CDs, computer software packages

Resources in and around your classroom

Immediate resources

Your classroom is an immediate source of learning materials. Many everyday objects can be used for measurement and data collection activities, and for developing number concepts and computation strategies. Examples include:
- parts of the classroom – floor, door, windows, board, and so on
- furniture – desks, chairs, cupboards, shelves, and so on
- students' possessions – pencils, rulers, pens, school bags, lunch boxes, and so on.

The school compound beyond your classroom is also a rich source of materials. Students can explore mathematical concepts such as symmetry by examining the school buildings, playground, plants and trees. The activities that take place within the school compound also provide learning opportunities. For example, students could carry out investigations to determine the most popular games, sports, lunch foods, and so on. Each school compound is different, so you should explore your school compound to determine how it can be used to teach mathematics.

A classroom bulletin board

A classroom bulletin board allows you to display work and share ideas. To set up a bulletin board, you may designate an area of wall space or use a board made of soft wood such as chipboard. Work together with your students to prepare and monitor the bulletin board displays. In Levels 1 to 3, you will need to take responsibility for maintaining the display. From Level 4 upwards, the students can take on more responsibility for preparing and maintaining the display. Use the bulletin board to:
- pose problems and puzzles
- explain solutions to displayed problems and puzzles
- elicit examples of concepts
- display the results of data-collection exercises
- display pictures and examples of how mathematics is used in real life (graphs, maps, and so on).

Your students may learn from the displays independently, in their own time. However, you should actively use the bulletin board by discussing the displays with the students, and using the discussions for informal assessment purposes.

Learning centres

You can also set up a learning centre in your classroom. The learning centre is an area where you store enrichment activities and materials at varying levels of difficulty. Check and comment on students' work and provide guidance for possible follow-up activities.

Building up a collection of materials

Students are most likely to use materials that are readily available in the classroom. So it is a good idea to build up a varied collection of learning materials for your classroom.

Selecting appropriate materials

When selecting materials, ask yourself the following questions:
- Are the materials directly related to the concepts or skills being developed?
- Do the materials facilitate the students' movement from one level of abstraction to another, for example, from the concrete to the abstract?
- Are the materials appropriate for the ages and developmental level of your students?
- Are the materials big/small enough for the students to use easily?
- Does the level of complexity of the materials match your students' mathematical development and needs?
- Are the materials challenging enough/easy enough?
- Will the materials stimulate the students' interest?

The following list gives you an idea of the types of materials that could be used in teaching the various content areas. Note that the list is not exhaustive and the assignment of materials to particular content areas is not definitive. Some materials are suitable for teaching a variety of content areas or topics, as necessary and when appropriate.

Content areas	Manipulative	Print materials	Games and puzzles	Technological devices
Technological devices	Common objects, e.g. buttons, seeds, stones, sticks, etc.; base ten blocks; place value charts or pockets; hundred charts; sorting trays; attribute blocks; sand boxes; Cuisenaire rods; abaci (counting frames); fraction sets	Numeral and base facts; flash cards; stories with a mathematical theme; number lines	Numeral jigsaw puzzles; colour-by-number puzzles; dominoes	Calculators
Measurement	Ruler; measuring tapes; clocks; watches and watch faces; measuring cylinders; cups; spoons; thermometers; balance and scales; various containers; string; trundle and wheel	Simple maps; calendars; squared paper		
Money	Coins; notes; play money notes	Advertisements		Calculators
Geometry	Models of 2D and 3D shapes; geo-board; tangram pieces; drinking straws; string; attribute blocks	Dots and squared paper	Battleship game	
Statistics and data handling	Building blocks; dice	Newspaper and magazine clippings of graphs; squared paper		

Acquiring materials

The quickest way to acquire materials is to buy them. However, this can be unnecessarily expensive. There are many inexpensive, effective ways of building up a collection of learning materials. Here are some suggestions:

- Collect manipulatives such as shells, seeds, stones, sticks, beads, and so on.
- Prepare your own fraction pieces from sheets of card or plastic.
- Prepare place value charts using Bristol board.
- Involve parents in constructing materials such as geo-boards, sets of 3D shapes, abaci, and so on.
- Involve students in constructing simple materials such as clock faces, tangram pieces, equivalent fraction charts, and so on.

If you decide to construct materials, first find a well-prepared commercial or local example of the material, note its mathematical properties, and ensure that these properties are features of your constructed materials. For example, when guiding your students to construct equivalent fraction charts, ensure that the fractional parts have been divided correctly.

Whether you purchase or construct your materials, ensure that they are attractive, durable and safe to use. Protect re-usable materials from damage so that they can be used repeatedly. Laminate materials such as charts and work cards, and store all materials in a cool, dry place. You can use cardboard boxes or inexpensive plastic bins as containers.

Using materials in the mathematics classroom

You can use materials in your classroom in several ways. For example, you could use materials to:

- facilitate the use of teaching methods such as guided discovery and co-operative learning groups
- provide enrichment activities
- cater for students' individual abilities and allow them to progress at different rates
- introduce new concepts
- initiate investigations
- generate discussions.

As far as possible and where appropriate, the students themselves should work with the materials – either on their own or with your guidance – in order to explore mathematical ideas. When you use the materials for demonstration or instruction purposes, make sure that you select materials that are large enough for the students to see easily.

Several factors influence how effectively the teaching or learning materials enhance students' learning. Some of these factors include:

- the students' readiness for the materials
- the quality of the materials
- the appropriateness of the materials for developing the mathematical ideas of the lesson.

Overleaf you will find some general and specific guidelines for using materials in your classroom.

General guidelines
- Check your supplies. Ensure that you have sufficient materials so that each student can have the quantity of materials necessary to develop the intended concept, skill or procedure.
- Plan properly. Before the lesson, select the materials you want to use, and plan how to integrate them into the lesson. Sometimes, during the lesson, you may find that students need other materials; adjust your lesson and include the use of other materials as necessary.
- Get to know the material. Acquaint yourself with the materials before introducing them to your students. If you are unfamiliar with the materials, practise using them yourself before the lesson. Preview print material, films, videos and computer software in order to identify the mathematical concepts and vocabulary that students should have acquired in order to use the materials successfully.
- Use a range of materials. There are a variety of ways to teach each mathematical concept, skill or procedure. For example, when students are learning about place value, they could use abaci, ice-cream sticks, base ten blocks, place value charts, and so on. The use of a variety of materials appeals to students' different interests and learning styles. Also, as students identify differences and similarities in the representations, they will gradually abstract the relevant mathematical ideas.
- Make sure students understand what to do with the materials. Let the students play with new or unfamiliar materials before you use them formally in a lesson. Ask questions to find out what they learned about the materials, and use these observations as a basis for the formal use of the materials in the classroom. Ensure that the students understand the purpose for using the materials and that they understand how to use them.
- Evaluate the use of the materials after each lesson. Ask yourself: Were the students motivated? Did they understand what to do with the materials? What difficulties, if any, arose during the lesson? Did the materials help to achieve the intended learning outcomes?

Guidelines for using manipulatives
- Monitor your students' progress. Allow them to work with manipulatives until they are ready to move onto semi-concrete or symbolic representations. Also remember that if you let students continue working with manipulatives for too long, they may become bored and demotivated. Always monitor your students' progress to determine the most appropriate time for them to move on to other representations.
- Ask questions. Encourage students to talk about what they are doing and understanding as they use manipulatives. You may use their comments for assessment purposes and to guide your lesson development.

Guidelines for using print materials
- Encourage your students to describe pictures, drawing and diagrams. They should identify components such as lines, shapes, labels, and so on. Encourage them to interpret and discuss the meanings of each component. For example, students should be able to discuss the various ways they could interpret a diagram such as the following:

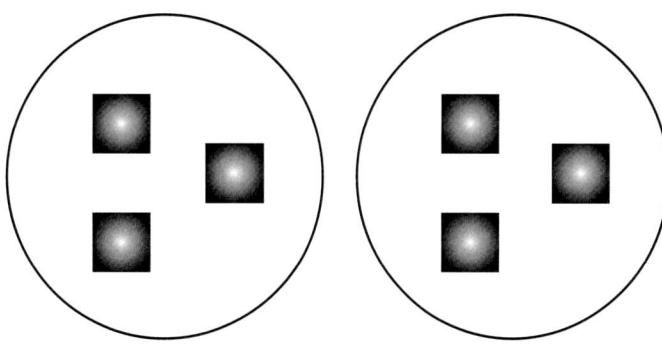

- Use print materials such as textbooks, pupil books, newspaper clippings, and so on for a variety of purposes. For example, students may use these materials as a source of information, for drills and practice exercises, or for checking generalisations that they have developed.
- Use manipulatives to help students gain an understanding of the mathematical ideas and the vocabulary that appears in the print material.
- Make sure that the language and instructions are clear, easy to use and pitched at the students' level of development. The mathematical language should always be used accurately, information should be well-spaced and easy-to-read, and pictures and diagrams should reinforce the ideas and make reading easier.

Guidelines for using games and puzzles

- Build up your collection of games and puzzles by encouraging students to develop their own games and puzzles. You can also develop new games by adapting the rules and actions of existing games.
- Each time you play a game, make sure students understand the rules.
- Monitor your students' progress during games. Check their use of mathematical concepts or skills required by the game. Note their strengths, weaknesses and misconceptions.
- During the game or puzzle session, discuss the students' responses with them. Encourage them to explain what they learned and to identify their difficulties. Follow up with appropriate activities to help them to improve.

Guidelines for using technological devices

- Prepare your students for using technological materials. Introduce the key ideas, concepts and vocabulary they will hear, see or use.
- Use follow-up activities to review, evaluate and reinforce the mathematical ideas used in the materials.

Using selected materials

The geo-board

A geo-board is a piece of board with an array of pegs or nails securely fastened to the board. Although the sizes of geo-boards may vary, an appropriate size for students is a 20 cm × 20 cm board with five rows of five nails or pegs (for younger students) or ten rows of ten nails or pegs (for older students). They can stretch rubber bands around the nails or pegs to make different kinds of shapes.

Geo-boards may help students develop and consolidate geometrical concepts related to plane shapes, for example polygons, curves, lines and symmetry.

Teaching and learning materials

Activities

- Ask students to make different types of shapes on their geo-boards and to describe them. For example:
- Make a four-sided figure. How many different four-sided figures can you make? Describe and name these shapes.
- Make a triangle with one right angle. Take another rubber band and make another triangle so that your first triangle changes to a rectangle. Explain what you did to make the rectangle.
- How many rectangles with an area of 24 square centimetres can you make on your geo-board? Write down the lengths of their sides.
- Make a quadrilateral whose area is the same as its perimeter. Describe your shape.

These types of activities could be followed up by activities involving drawing shapes on dotted, square, graph or plain paper.

Tangram puzzles

Tangram puzzles are made up of seven shapes cut from a square piece of paper, as shown here. Use heavy paper such as cardboard or Bristol board. If these are unavailable, use plain paper. You should provide younger students with the pieces; older students may make their own.

Instructions for making tangram pieces

- Start with a square piece of paper.
- Fold the square in half to make two triangles. Mark the fold line with a pencil or crayon. Cut along the fold line.
- Take one of the triangles and fold it in half to make two smaller triangles (A and B). Cut along the fold. Set aside the two triangles.

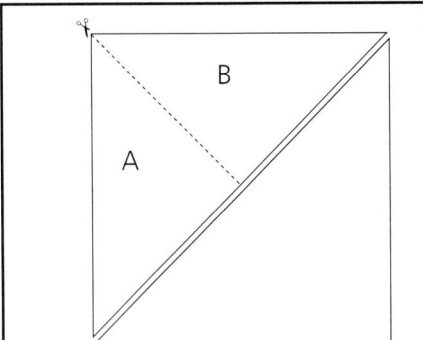

- Take the other large triangle (C). Place the cut edge horizontally. Take the top point and fold it down until it touches the middle of the long cut edge. Open it again. The fold should make a small triangle at the top of the paper. Cut along the fold as shown in the picture. Then place this small triangle with your other two completed pieces.

- Place the remaining piece on your desk. Fold it in half and cut along the fold line as shown.

- Take one of the halves. Turn your paper so that the longest side is on the bottom. Place this side on your desk. Fold the longest side so that you get a square and a triangle (D and E). Cut along the fold line. Set aside these pieces with your other completed pieces.

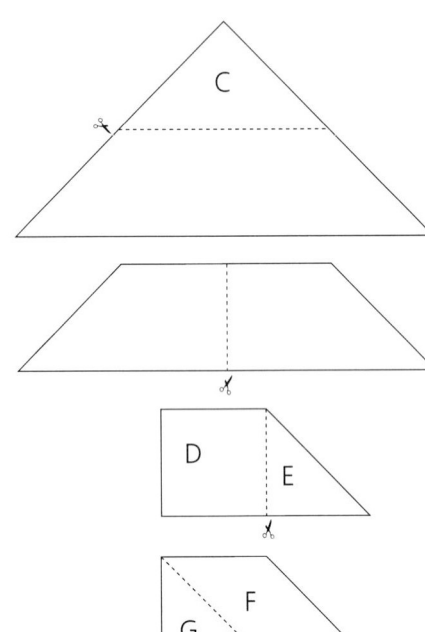

- Take the remaining piece and fold it so that the 90 degree angle touches the angle opposite it (F and G). Cut along the fold line.

- You should now have the seven pieces of the tangram puzzle.

Activities

- Put the pieces back to form the original square.
- Name the shapes of each of the seven pieces.

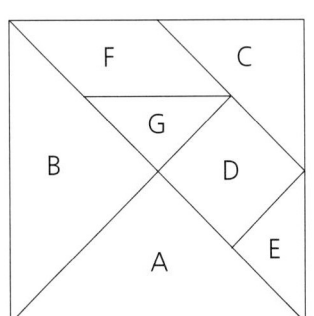

Teaching and learning materials

- Make other geometrical shapes, using a combination of the pieces. For example: make a triangle using two triangular pieces – E and G; make a square using three of the pieces – C, G and E; make a rectangle using four triangles and one quadrilateral – A, B, F, E and G.
- Make everyday shapes such as a boat, or a bird, using all or some of the pieces.

Worksheets

You may design worksheets in such a way that they are self-correcting. For example, you could have a puzzle in a worksheet. As the students attempt to solve the puzzle, they would get an indication as to whether their responses to the tasks are correct. If they solve the puzzle, their responses are most likely correct. The puzzle may take the form of words or phrases that the students have to complete. An example is given below.

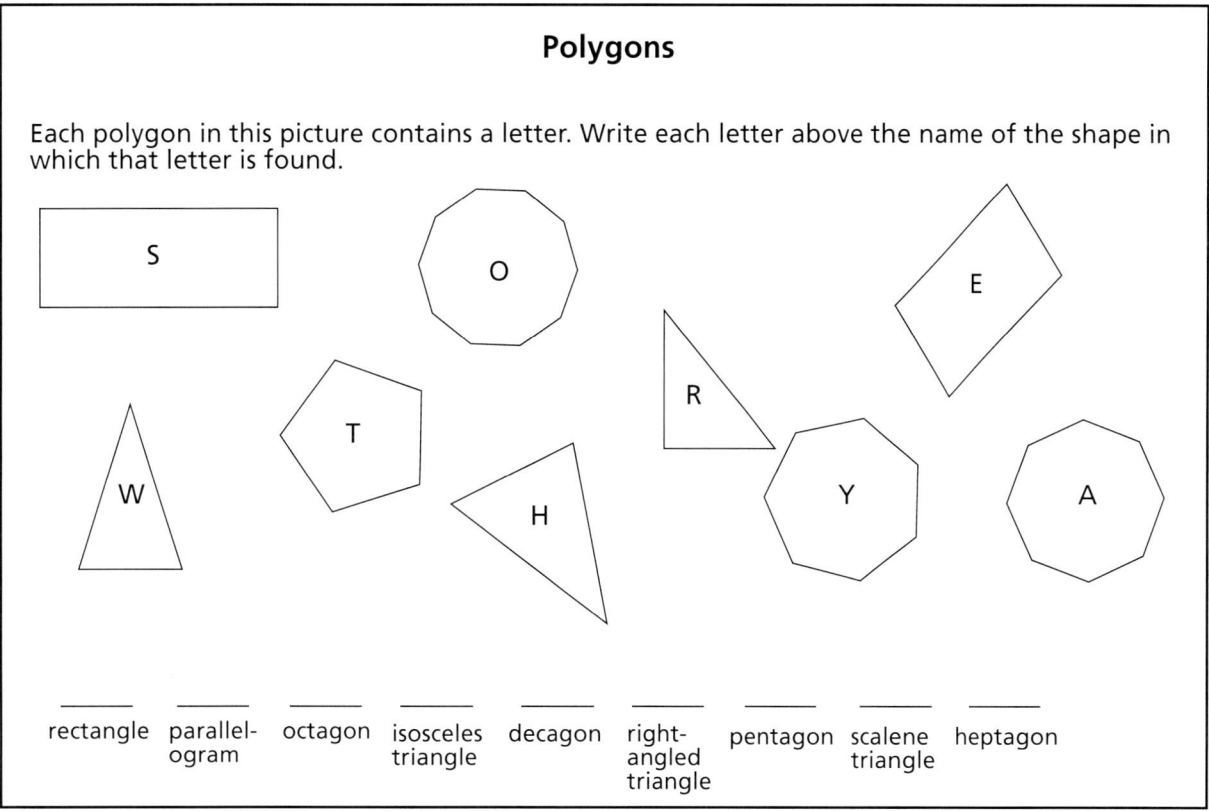

Calculators

Use calculators for the following purposes:
- to investigate concepts and problems requiring computation strategies beyond the students' level
- to build up strategies for recalling basic facts
- to study real-life situations.

Activities

Help your students to understand the functions of the calculator keys. For example, you could ask the students to press a key or a series of keys and note what happens on the display. Let them discuss whether their calculators operate in different ways.

You can use calculators with younger students to help them practise counting. Ask the students to key in 1 + = = = ... and to note what happens. Some calculators might require the following sequence for counting: 1 + + = = ... As the students progress to skip counting and counting backwards, let them speculate as to how their calculators will perform these functions. Then they should check the accuracy of their speculations.

Use calculator games to help develop students' reasoning skills. Two examples are outlined below.
- Students can work in pairs. Each student keys a number, for example 25, into his or her calculator. Each student then uses any combination of the four operations (+, −, ×, ÷) to get an answer of 0. Multiplication by 0 and division by 0 are not allowed. The student who gets to 0 using the fewest operations is the winner.
- Students work in pairs using one calculator per pair. They key in a number, for example 100. The first player subtracts any number from 1 to 9 (including 1 and 9). The second player does the same, this time subtracting from the difference that is on the display. The players alternate turns. If a player subtracts a number to get 0, that player loses the game.

Calculators allow students to explore calculations involving the four basic operations. The following are some related activities.
- Let students use their calculators to multiply a set of numbers by 10, 100 and 1 000. Let them record their answers, then examine the results for any patterns that would provide a way of obtaining the answers without the calculator. This activity can be extended to multiplication and division of decimals.
- Write a multiplication statement on the board, such as $5 \times 13 \times 7$. Let the students use their calculators to find the answers. Multiply one of the factors in the statement above by 3, for example $5 \times 13 \times 21$. Let the students find the answer using their calculators. Record the answer. Let them find the answers to the other two possible cases: $15 \times 13 \times 7$ and $5 \times 39 \times 7$. Repeat using other statements and multiplication by other numbers. Ask the class for their observations. Let students explain what would happen to the product of a set of numbers if any one number in the set were multiplied by another factor. Guide the students to explore how the product would be affected if every number in the set were multiplied by the same number.

References and further reading

Anthony, G. (1996). 'Active learning in a constructivist framework', *Educational Studies in Mathematics*, 41 (3), 3–11.

Grossnickle, F.E., Reckzeh, J., Perry, L.M. & Ganoe, N.S. (1983). *Discovering meanings in elementary school mathematics* (7th ed.), New York: Holt, Rinehart & Winston.

Lemlech, J.K. (1998). *Curriculum and instructional methods for the elementary and middle school* (4th ed.), Upper Saddle River, NJ: Merrill.

Sheffield, L. & Cruikshank, D.E. (2000). *Teaching and learning elementary and middle school mathematics* (4th ed.), New York: John Wiley.

Unit-by-unit support

Units 1 and 2 Tens and ones

Materials
- popsicle sticks
- rubber bands

Objectives

Students should be able to:

- ✓ identify and complete number patterns and sequences
- ✓ identify place value in three- and four-digit numbers
- ✓ tell the total value of any digit in two- and three-digit numbers
- ✓ work with hundreds, tens and ones
- ✓ distinguish between place value and total value.

Suggested approach

tens	ones

Tally chart

Draw a tally chart on the board, as shown on the left. Display a popsicle stick. Ask: How many sticks? (One.) Put a tally in the chart. Continue to display different numbers of sticks: three sticks, four sticks, five sticks, and so on. Then explain that we can make a bundle of ten sticks; put a rubber band around ten sticks. Explain that 10 ones are equal to 1 ten. Write a tally in the tens column to show one ten.

Let students work in pairs to make bundles of sticks with single sticks to illustrate two-digit numbers with one ten. For example: Ten sticks (one bundle) + three single sticks = 13. Do more examples, such as 14, 15, etc. Then do the same for two-digit numbers with more than one ten, such as 35, 42, etc.

Explain to the students the difference between place value and total value. Write the number 945 on the board. Ask the students what the total value of this number is. They should be able to tell you that it is nine hundred and forty-five. Tell them that we know this because each digit has a value that depends on its position in the number. In this example, 9 is in the place value of hundreds, 4 is in the place value of tens, and 5 is in the place value of units. Now write 459 on the board. Explain that although this number contains the same digits as 945, it has a different total value because the place value of the digits is different. Ask a student to say what the place value of each digit is.

Let students complete Units 1 and 2 in their Pupil Books. You may need to revise the signs <, > and = for the second question in Unit 1.

Units 3 and 4 Place values and numbers to 999

Materials
- place-value charts
- flash cards labelled 100, 10, 1 (ten of each)
- flash cards with numerals and number names for a range of two- and three-digit numbers
- pins or sticky putty to put up flash cards

Objectives

Students should be able to:

 write numbers up to 999 on place-value charts

 write numerals for numbers up to 999.

Suggested approach

Stick up the following flash cards or draw the numbers on the board:

| 100 | 100 | 100 | 10 | 10 | 1 | 1 | 1 | 1 | 1 | 1 |

h	t	o

Next to the numbers, stick up or draw a place-value chart, as shown on the left.

Ask the class: How many hundreds are there? (Three.) Ask a student to write 3 in the hundreds column. How many tens are there? (Two.) Ask a student to write 2 in the tens column. How many ones are there? (Six.) Ask a student to write 6 in the ones column. The place-value chart should now look like the one shown on the left.

h	t	o
3	2	6

Ask a student to come to the front of the class. Give them a few hundreds, tens and ones cards – for example five hundreds, four tens and nine ones. The student should count each set of cards, draw a place-value chart on the board and fill in the correct numerals under each column. Get the class to check the answer. Repeat this procedure with a few other students, using different numbers of cards each time. Make sure there are fewer than ten of each set – hundreds, tens and ones. Sometimes you may give the student no tens or ones, and they must fill in a zero under the relevant column. When you feel that the students are confident working with place value in this way, let them work through Unit 3 on their own.

Unit 4 follows a similar principle to Unit 3, although students have to work with number names as well as numerals. If you wish, repeat a similar procedure to that described above. Also use the flash cards with numerals and number names. Show a student a card with a three-digit number, and ask them to write the number name on the board. Repeat this with different students and different numbers. Reverse the procedure: show the number name and get the student to write the numeral. After going through a few examples, let the students work through Unit 4.

Unit 5 Ordering numbers

Materials
- hundred chart

Objectives

Students should be able to:
- ✓ identify numbers before or after a given number
- ✓ order numbers from smallest to largest and vice versa
- ✓ identify and complete number patterns and sequences.

Suggested approach

Show the class the hundred chart. Point to different numbers and ask students what numbers they are. Also get students to come up and point to different numbers that you call out. Show students that the number that comes after 23 is 24 (by pointing on the hundred chart). Repeat for other examples. Ask: What number comes after 42? 36? etc. Repeat the process to show students what number comes before a given number.

Write a sequence of numbers on the board, with some numbers missing, for example: 12, 13, ___, ___, 16. Ask individual students to fill in the missing numbers. Repeat this with sets of larger numbers. Write some sets of numbers on the board, with three numbers in a set. Ask individual students to identify the largest and smallest numbers in each set. Students can complete the exercises in Unit 5. Teachers in Jamaica should also get students to identify the largest and smallest numbers in sets of three-digit numbers.

Units 6 to 9 Addition and subtraction

Materials
- bottle caps for each student
- sweets
- popsicle sticks or straws
- four short lengths of twine per student
- tally charts for each pair of students
- large tally chart for the board

Objectives

Children should be able to:
- ✓ add a two-digit number to a single-digit number without regrouping
- ✓ subtract a single-digit number from a two-digit number without regrouping.

Suggested approach

Tell the class you have five sweets, but you want eight. Ask: How many more sweets must I add to five so I have eight? Put five sweets in your hand. Illustrate the solution by adding sweets one by one to the sweets in your hand, getting the students to count the sweets after each addition, until you have eight. Ask: How many sweets did we add? Get a student to come to the board and write the number sentence: 5 + 3 = 8.

Unit-by-unit support 21

Give out nine bottle caps to each student. Tell them to put four bottle caps in one hand. Ask: How many more bottle caps do you need to make nine altogether? Let them solve the problem practically.

Repeat the practical activity, using different examples. Also use this activity to illustrate the relationship between addition and subtraction. For example, you could say: 3 + 5 = 8. How many do I have to take away from eight to get five? Let students practise addition and subtraction, using the bottle caps. Then let them complete Unit 6.

Begin with this word problem: I have two bunches of flowers. One bunch has 14 flowers, and the other bunch has 15 flowers. How many flowers are there altogether?

Ask students how they would solve this problem. Hand out the popsicle sticks or straws and twine, and ask students to work in pairs to represent the numbers as tens and ones. Ask one of the pairs to illustrate how we can represent 15 as one ten and five ones, and 14 as one ten and four ones. Draw up the numbers on the tally chart. Ask: How many tens altogether? How many ones altogether? After they have given the answers, show how we represent the answer as a number. If you wish, let the students work through more examples of adding two-digit numbers without regrouping. Then let students complete Units 7 and 8 in their Pupil Books.

Again, use sticks or straws. Get students to represent the number 35 in tens and ones, using the bundles of ten sticks as tens and loose sticks as ones. Then ask them to take away four from 35. They should demonstrate practically using the bundles (tens) and loose sticks (ones). Fill in each step on the tally chart on the board.

Write a word problem on the board, for example:

- Joan has 47 bags. She sells 5. How many does she have left?

Let students work out the answer using their materials. Then let them work through Unit 9 in their Pupil Books.

Units 10 and 11   Working with numbers

Materials
- calculators

Objectives

Students should be able to:

 identify the place value and total value of any digit in two- and three-digit numbers

 use a calculator to carry out calculations when necessary

 read numbers up to 999

 write numbers up to 999 in words and symbols.

Suggested approach

Go though the example at the top of Unit 10 on the board. The students should now be familiar with the difference between place value

and total value. Write a few more examples on the board, for example:
9 groups of 100, 3 groups of 10 and 1 group of ones
5 groups of 100 and 2 groups of ones

For each example, ask a student to come to the board and fill in the tally boxes. Do not rub these examples out. Then let the students work through Unit 10.

For each of the examples on the board, ask the students to enter that number into their calculators. They can show their partners to make sure that they are doing it correctly.

Write three numbers on the board, for example 656, 221, 937. Ask the students how they know which is the greatest number and which is the smallest. Explain that they first need to look at the hundreds place value, then at the tens place value, and finally at the units place value. So in this example, 937 is the greatest number as it has the highest number in the hundreds place value. Repeat with a number of examples.

The 'talk about' box in Unit 11 asks students to think about where we use machines to help us work with numbers. We use machines (such as calculators and computers) to help us to work out more complicated problems.

Ask students to work through the questions in Unit 11.

Units 12 and 13 Measuring

Materials
- rulers
- metre rule
- items to measure such as twine, tape, books, matchboxes, and so on

Objectives

Students should be able to:

 estimate, measure and record lengths using standard and non-standard units of measurement

 explain why there is a need for a smaller unit of measure – the centimetre

 compare linear measurements of two or three objects.

Suggested approach

Hold up an exercise book and a matchbox. Ask: How many matchboxes long do you think this exercise book measures? Write students' different guesses on the board. Then check the actual length by placing the matchboxes side by side and counting them. Let the students work in pairs or small groups to measure different objects using non-standard units (matches, straws, and so on).

Write the words 'centimetre' and 'metre' on the board. Explain that although it is useful to use real objects such as straws and matchboxes for measuring, we have standard units that we use for measuring lengths. Ask students if they can name some of these units. If necessary, explain that we use the metric system. The standard unit of length is a metre. Invite students to explain the relationship between millimetres, centimetres, metres and kilometres. Show students the abbreviations for each of these units. Ask students to give suggestions of what would be measured in each unit.

Ask students why we need smaller units of measure such as the centimetre and why we cannot measure everything in metres. They should realise that they need smaller units of measure to measure objects that are smaller then a metre. You could ask them to measure themselves using the metre rule. This will help them see that centimetres allow them to take measurements accurately, otherwise they would have to say things like 'I am a little bit shorter than 1 metre.'

Ask three students to measure the length of something in the classroom. Write the name of the objects and their lengths on the board. Ask another student to come to the board and write the lengths in order, from shortest to longest. Repeat this activity, asking the students to measure the lengths of different objects in the classroom.

Get students to work through Units 12 and 13 in their Pupil Books.

If some students complete the questions and activities early, you may want to give them a few examples to convert between units. For example:

5 000 m = _____ km, 250 cm = _____ m, 1 000 mm = _____ m

Units 14 to 18 Data

Materials
- chart showing children's favourite fruits

Objectives

Students should be able to:

- explain what a tally chart is
- explain how to use tallies to construct a table
- use tally charts to organise collected data
- identify and describe situations in everyday life that involve data collection and data representation, and say why people collect data
- draw and interpret simple pictographs
- read information from a pictograph
- collect and represent data
- describe the characteristics of bar graphs in which one block represents one unit of data
- compare sets using <, > and = signs.

Suggested approach

Ask the students if they can think of any examples in real life where people would want to collect data (for example a company might want to find out which flavour sweets children liked). Explain the idea of a government census.

Write three different team games in a tally table on the board, for example: rounders, football, cricket. Tell the students each to choose their favourite out of the three games. Ask the students who chose cricket to put up their hands. Ask a student to count how many students have their hands up. Tell them that we can show this information on a tally chart. Students worked with tallies in Level 2, but they might need reminding of how to draw the tally marks. Ask a student to come to the board and fill in the tallies for the number of students who chose cricket as their favourite sport. Repeat the process for rounders and football.

Ask the students how they could use the information in the tally chart to make a table. Ask them what they would need to show in the table. Ask a student to come and draw the outline of the table on the board and to fill in the name of the sports. Ask the students to then fill in the numbers in the table.

Ask the students to complete Unit 14.

Now, ask all the students who chose cricket to come to the front of the class and stand in a line. Then get those who chose rounders and football to come to the front, each group in a line. Ask: Which line is the longest? Which is the most popular game? How could we represent this 'human' graph on the board?

Suggest using a stick figure to represent each pupil. Draw a pictograph on the board to represent how many students chose each game. Get the students to advise how many stick figures to draw, what each axis should be labelled, and so on.

Do a similar activity to find out students' favourite subjects. This time, get students to raise their hands to indicate their choices, instead of standing in rows. Draw the pictograph on the board.

Display a pictograph of fruit picked by four children, for example:

Child	Number of mangoes
Sam	🥭🥭🥭🥭🥭
Amanda	🥭🥭🥭
Nadia	🥭🥭🥭🥭🥭🥭🥭
Jeremy	🥭🥭🥭

Ask questions about the pictograph, for example: Who picked the most mangoes? How many mangoes did she pick? Which two children picked the same number of mangoes? How many did they pick altogether? Who picked the least mangoes? What was the total number of mangoes picked by the four children?

Then get students to work through Units 15 and 16 in their Pupil Books.

The 'talk about' box in Unit 15 asks students to think about why it is important to recycle tins. You may want to ask students to research this. Or, tell them that it is very expensive and harmful to the environment to keep digging the materials needed to make tins from the ground. It is much cheaper (and better for the environment) to collect used tins and make them into new ones again. Companies could pay people to go around and collect all the used and unwanted tins and deliver them to the company.

Unit-by-unit support

Explain to the students that a block graph is another way of showing information. Tell them that they are going to show the information in the pictograph of the fruit picked by Sam, Amanda, Nadia and Jeremy in a block graph.

Draw the outline of a block graph that is similar to the one in Unit 17. Label the y-axis 'Number of mangoes picked' and write in the scale. Label the x-axis 'Child' and write in the names of the children. Ask the students what each part of the graph shows. Explain that each block represents one piece of information.

Ask a student how many mangoes Sam picked. (5.) Ask another student how they could represent this on the graph. (By colouring in five blocks in the 'Sam' column.) Ask the student to come and colour these blocks in. Continue until the block graph is completed.

Go through the example at the top of Unit 17 with the students, before asking them to complete the questions on this page.

Remind students of the signs <, > and =. Draw two sets on the board – one set of three apples and another set of five apples. Ask a student to come up and fill in the correct sign – less than, greater than or equal to. Do this with a few more examples. If some students struggle to distinguish the less than and greater than sign, you can draw a simple sketch of a crocodile, and say that they should imagine the sign is the mouth of the hungry crocodile – it will always open towards the bigger set.

Get students to work through Unit 18 in their Pupil Books.

Unit 19 Review and assessment

Materials
- calendar

Objectives

Students should be able to:

 work with calendars

 solve problems involving addition and subtraction of whole numbers

Suggested approach

The first part of Unit 19 reviews work on calendars, days and months. Students have covered this work in previous levels. To refresh their memories, show students a calendar showing the present month and ask questions about it, for example: What day of the week does the first day of this month fall on? How many days are in this month? How many days did the last month have? How many Sundays are there in this month? Who has a birthday in this month? When is the next national holiday? How many weeks and days is it from today? and so on. Then let students work through page 23 in their Pupil Books.

The second part of Unit 19 reviews work done earlier on problem-solving skills involving addition and subtraction of whole numbers.

Let students work through the questions on their own. You may wish to use this as an assessment activity.

Unit 20   Ordinal numbers

Materials
- fifteen different objects

Objectives:
Students should be able to:
- ✓ identify the ordinal position of an object in an arranged set
- ✓ identify the object that is in a given ordinal position in an arranged set.

Suggested approach

Lay out the objects in a row. Describe the position of each object. For example, the pen is first in the line, the eraser is second, the apple is third, and so on.

Students learnt about ordinal numbers in Kindergarten, so this should be revision for them. Ask the students questions about the line of objects, for example:

- In which position is the pencil?
- What object is in the ninth position?

Ask the students to complete the questions in Unit 20.

Units 21 and 22   Fractions

Materials
- circular and rectangular cut-outs of different sizes
- objects such as bottle caps, shells, seeds, etc.

Objectives:
Students should be able to:
- ✓ identify the fraction of a whole or set
- ✓ represent fractions using numbers or pictures.

Suggested approach

In Units 21 and 22, students work with the following fractions: $\frac{1}{2}$, $\frac{1}{4}$ and $\frac{1}{3}$. Begin with halves. Give each student a blank circular cut-out. Ask them to fold their circles in half and to write the symbol for one-half on each half of the circle. Emphasise that the two parts are equal.

Show students the circular cut-outs divided into four equal parts (quarters). Ask: What do you notice about each of the four parts? (They are equal.) Fold the circular cut-out in half. Ask how many quarters make up each half. Ask the students to fold their own cut-outs in half again, to make four equal parts. Let them use crayons to shade $\frac{1}{2}$ of the cut-out. Emphasise that two quarters make up one half.

Unit-by-unit support   27

Let students count out a group of four objects. Establish that this is one whole set of four. Ask students to open out their circular cut-outs, and to divide their groups of four objects into two equal groups so that each group is on one half of the circle. Explain that they have divided the set of objects into two equal parts. Each part is equal to 1/2 of the set. Repeat this exercise using other sets.

Let students work through Unit 21 in their Pupil Books.

In Unit 22 students work with the fraction $1/3$. Give each student a rectangular cut-out. Show them how to divide their rectangles into three equal parts. Emphasise that the three parts are equal.

Go through the introduction to Unit 22 with the students. Introduce the terms numerator and denominator. Remind the students that the numerator tells us the number of parts we are working with and the denominator tells us the total number of parts in the whole.

Draw three circles on the board. Ask a student to come and colour in $1/3$ of them. Next draw six circles on the board and ask another student to colour in $1/3$ of them. Students may have trouble with this, but show them that they can divide the six circles into two groups of three.

Now let students work through Unit 22 in their Pupil Books.

Units 23 to 25 Time

Materials
- a large teacher-made clock with movable hands
- a real clock
- smaller teacher-made clocks – one per pupil
- a clock stamp

Objectives:

Students should be able to:

 represent time in different ways

 read time off an analogue clock to the hour, half-hour and quarter-hour.

Suggested approach

Set the clock to show half past seven. Ask: Which number tells us the hour? (Seven.) Which number tells us how many minutes past the hour? (6.) Point out that we can also call this time 'seven thirty'. Show the students how to write 7:30. Repeat with similar examples, such as 3:30, 10:30, 12:30 and 1:30. Let some of the students take turns to set the hands of the clock. Write the corresponding notation on the board, and read the time aloud.

Draw a circle on the board, and draw lines dividing it into quarters. Ask the students what we call each of the four equal parts. (A quarter.) Ask a student to come up to the board and shade a quarter. Then ask another student to shade another quarter of the same shape. Ask:

- How many quarters are shaded? (Two.)
- How much of the whole shape is unshaded? (Two quarters.)
- What is another way of saying two quarters? (One half.)

Draw the students' attention to the fact that the circle is now divided into two equal parts.

Go back to the circle divided into quarters on the board. Write '$\frac{1}{4}$' in each quadrant. Now hold up a clock face, and slowly move the minute hand through the first quadrant of the hour, from the hour mark to the quarter past the hour mark. Explain that when the minute hand points to the 3, the time is quarter past the hour. Continue moving the minute hand through the second quadrant to the half past mark. Explain that when the minute hand points to the 6, the time is half past the hour. Continue moving the minute hand through the third quadrant, and explain the concept of 'a quarter to' the hour. Move the clock hands to a variety of times involving quarter to, quarter past and half past. Point out that as the minute hand moves, the hour hand also moves, although it does so at a slower pace. Demonstrate this on a real clock, and pay attention to the position of the hour hand when the minute hand is on 3, 6 or 9. Draw a variety of times on the board, and get the students to read the time, explaining how they worked out the time according to the positions of the minute and hour hands. Each student should write the time on the board, using the following kind of notation: $\frac{1}{4}$ past 2, $\frac{1}{4}$ to 5, half past 6, and so on. Then let them use their clock faces to show $\frac{1}{4}$ to, or $\frac{1}{4}$ past, the hour for various times.

Use the clock face to stamp blank clock faces into students' exercise books, and ask them to write in given times, for example: 12:30, 11:00, 8:30, and so on.

Let students work through Units 23 and 24 in their Pupil Books.

Turn to Pupil Book page 29. Read through the information at the top half of the page. Let the students count in fives again to reach 60. Then let them work through the unit, working in pairs. Remind them to use the pictures of the drops to help them count how many minutes are represented by each fraction of an hour.

Units 26 and 27   Review and assessment

Objectives:

Students should be able to:

-  read and write time notation
- 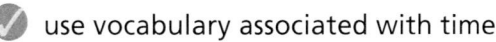 use vocabulary associated with time
-  work with counting, basic operations (+ and -) and units of measurements
- read and interpret information presented on a pictograph
- identify fractions of a whole or a set.

Suggested approach

Unit 26 reviews work just covered on reading and writing time on analogue faces. Check students' work to make sure that they understand that the short hand represents hours and the long hand

Unit-by-unit support   29

represents minutes. They should also be able to draw the hands clearly, using the correct positions for times on the hour, half-hour and quarter-hour. Also check the spelling of numbers as well as 'quarter', 'half' and 'o'clock'.

The first page of Unit 27 can be used to assess students' ability to work with counting, basic operations (addition and subtraction) and units of measurement. Encourage students to check their work to make sure they have counted accurately. If any students are having difficulty with basic operations, give them more written examples to use for practice. For activity 3, remind students that they should think about measuring the real object, not the pictures! They are not, in fact, expected to measure the items – only to select the appropriate unit of measurement.

The second page of Unit 27 can be used to assess work thus far on pictographs, fractions and time.

Units 28 to 31   Addition and subtraction

Materials
- about 50 popsicle sticks
- thread or rubber bands
- tally cards for each pair of students
- large tally chart for the board

Objectives
Students should be able to:
- ✓ add two-digit numbers without regrouping
- ✓ subtract a one-digit number from a two-digit number with regrouping
- ✓ subtract a two-digit number from another two-digit number with and without regrouping
- ✓ add two-digit numbers to one- or two-digit numbers with regrouping.

Suggested approach

Revise the basic facts of addition and subtraction by giving simple addition and subtraction problems for students to answer orally. Let them work through Unit 28 in their Pupil Books to revise addition and subtraction without regrouping.

The 'talk about' box on this page asks the students about the relationship between adding and subtracting. Students should realise that the order of the numbers in an addition do not affect the answer, but it does in a subtraction. Also, in the groups of sums on this page, students should be able to see that they can use subtraction to check an addition and an addition to check a subtraction.

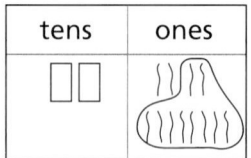

Give some simple word sums, for example:

- Mr Simon sold 24 boxes of bananas. His son sold eight boxes. How many boxes did they sell altogether?

```
  24
+  8
----
  32
```

Let the students use the popsicle sticks and tally charts to represent tens and ones as they solve the problem. Show them how to write the problem vertically and let a student fill in the answer.

30   Unit-by-unit support

Repeat a similar addition for 18 and 7. Emphasise that you exchange ten ones for one ten. Let the students use the popsicle sticks and tally charts to help them solve the questions in Unit 29.

Write a problem such as:

- Mary picks 17 mangoes. Laura picks 15 mangoes. How many mangoes did they pick altogether?

Follow the same procedure as above, this time adding a two-digit number to a two-digit number with regrouping.

Let the students use the popsicle sticks and tally charts to help them solve the questions in Unit 30.

Get each student to make a bundle of ten sticks, fastened tightly with a rubber band or thread. While they make these bundles, draw a tally chart on the board. Label the columns 'tens' and 'ones'. Ask some students how many sticks they have in their bundles (ten). Ask one student to put their bundle on a table and to call out 'ten'. Make a mark in the tens column of the tally chart to indicate that there is now one bundle of ten sticks on the table. A second student can bring his or her bundle forward and call out 'twenty'. Make a second mark in the tens column of the tally chart.

Continue in this way until the tenth student comes forward, puts down a bundle and calls out 'one hundred'. Ask the students how many tens make a hundred. (Ten tens.) Use the bundles to illustrate that one ten equals ten; two tens equal twenty; three tens equal thirty, and so on until ten tens equal a hundred. Write on the board: 10 tens = 100.

Ask several students to read this aloud. Then point to the tally marks in the tens column, and explain that ten tens make a hundred. Point out that we can make another column for hundreds. The tally chart should now look like the one on the left.

Demonstrate making a hundred by tying together ten bundles. Rub out the ten marks in the tens column of the tally chart and replace them with a single tally mark in the hundreds column.

Unwrap the bundle of a hundred and give back the bundles of ten. Repeat the above demonstration, but get students to show how many tens make a hundred and how to represent it on the tally chart.

Get students to place their bundles on the table. Again, they should call out the new total with each addition of ten and fill in the tally chart. However, this time, go up to 200. Pause to demonstrate the meaning of 200 in the same way as you did for 100. Continue until all students' bundles are on the table. Finish the exercise by getting students to remove their bundles, counting backwards and erasing a tally mark as each bundle is removed. Let students work through Unit 31 in their Pupil Books.

CD-Rom activity
- Number operations

Units 32 and 33 Numbers

Materials
- about 50 popsicle sticks
- thread
- bottle caps
- paper bags
- 20 to 30 matchboxes
- 200 to 300 spent matches

Objectives
Students should be able to:
- ✓ work with hundreds, tens and units
- ✓ order and compare numbers up to 999
- ✓ skip count in 5s, 10s, 20s, 25s, 100s
- ✓ add 100s.

Suggested approach

Ask a group of students to stand in a row, holding their bundles of sticks. Ask one of the other students to walk along the row, touching each bundle and counting in tens as they go. They should then write the number of sticks on the board. Repeat this several times; after a while, the student should not need to touch the bundles of sticks. They should count the number of students in the row and say immediately how many sticks they are holding: nine children – 90 sticks, and so on. You may want to develop the procedure slowly over several lessons until the skill has been mastered.

Hold up a card with a three-digit numeral, for example 120, written on it. Ask one of the students to go around the class touching enough bundles of sticks (in this case twelve) to make that number. As they touch each bundle, the student to whom it belongs should hold it up so that eventually everyone can see how many bundles of ten make 120. Repeat several times.

Ask a student to follow these steps:

- Come forward and cover the board with crosses.
- Draw rings around sets of ten crosses until all sets of ten are circled. There may be some crosses left over.
- Point to each of the sets, counting aloud in tens up to one hundred.
- Draw a bigger ring around all the rings counted so far (ten tens).
- Say how many crosses are in the big ring.
- Continue counting the rings of ten crosses.

If, for example, there are 134 crosses on the board, the student will stop after another three sets of ten. Ask: How many crosses are in the big ring? (100.) How many more crosses are in the other rings? (30.) Are there more than 130 crosses on the board? (Yes.) How many more? (4.)

Point out that there are a hundred and thirty, and four. Ask: What number do you think that is? (One hundred and thirty-four.) Demonstrate how the number is written.

Students can work through Unit 32 in their Pupil Books.

Students have already counted in tens. Give them some practice at skip counting with other numbers – twos, threes, fives, sevens, and so on, before letting them work through Unit 33 in their Pupil Books.

Unit-by-unit support

Additional activities

Skip counting in 100s

Students in OECS and Trinidad need to skip count in 100s. Teachers can use number lines to demonstrate how to count in 100s. Practise skip counting in 100s orally with students. Use this exercise to develop students' concept of numbers to a thousand. One way of introducing hundreds and thousands is through the concept of money: explain that a hundred cents is equal to $1. Ask students how many cents are in $2, $3, and so on. When you get to $10, write on the board: $10 = 1 000c. You can then go through $20, $30, and so on, to get students to count in thousands.

Adding 100s to 100s

Students in Trinidad also need to add hundreds to hundreds. Write the following example on the board: 200 + 300.

Write the sum in columns and ask the students to add – first units, then tens, then hundreds. Then give some more examples for students to work through, for example:

a   100 + 400   b   600 + 200
c   700 + 100   d   100 + 100 + 300

Now, write the following example on the board: 275 + 300.

Ask students how this sum differs from the previous additions of hundreds (275 is made up of hundreds, tens and units, not only hundreds). Demonstrate how to solve the sum, then let students solve a few more examples on the board. You can use the following examples for drilling:

a   192 + 300   b   489 + 500   c   568 + 200
d   148 + 300   e   599 + 200   f   382 + 300

Units 34 and 35   Money

Materials
- coins that are in circulation
- play coins or real coins for the students to use
- small items costing less than $1.00

Objectives

Students should be able to:

 identify the coins in circulation

 solve problems involving money

 make amounts using different combinations of coins.

Suggested approach

Show the students the coins that are in circulation. Ask the students to tell you which coin is which and to describe the main distinguishing features of each coin.

Let the students work in pairs. Write several combinations of coins on the board. Ask the students to use their coins to make the combinations. Let students say the total amount, for example:

  (10c) = 45c

Unit-by-unit support   33

Draw this on the chalkboard:

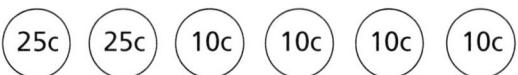

Let the students say the amount shown. Let them say the change if the following amounts are spent: 50c, 60c, 70c, 75c.

Write the following problem on the board:

- Jill had:

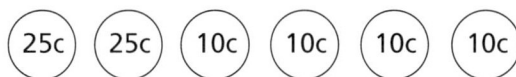

She bought a lollipop for 35c. How much did she have left?

Let the students act out the problem, using real or play money to find the answer. Provide two or three more examples. Let students work through Unit 34 in their Pupil Books.

The 'talk about' box in Unit 34 invites students to think about what they spend their money on. Expect answers such as food, drinks, bus fare and so on.

Draw these coins on the board:

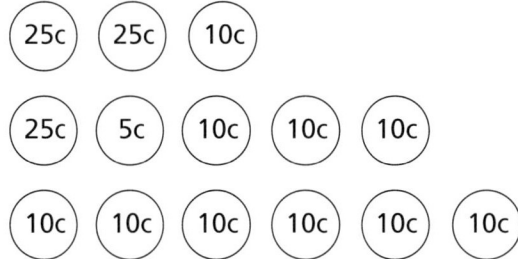

Ask the students to say the total amount in each set of coins. (60c.) Ask how the sets are different. Write on the board: 40c. Let the students use coins to show different ways of making this amount. Repeat with other examples.

Write on the board: 25c. Ask students to use three coins to make this amount. Repeat with other examples, such as: make 40c using four coins; make 40c using three coins.

Write this problem on the board:

- Harry had 25c, 10c, 10c, 10c, 10c, 10c, 10c. He bought bananas for 75c. How much money did he have left?

Let students act out the problem to find the answer. Repeat with other examples. Then get students to work through Unit 35.

Unit 36 Assessment

Objectives

Students should be able to:
- ✓ add two-digit numbers with and without regrouping
- ✓ skip count
- ✓ work with money.

Suggested approach

Use Unit 36 as a revision and assessment exercise to go over work covered in Units 28 to 35. Question 1 revises addition with regrouping. Make sure that students remember that they must carry over to the tens column. If necessary, give them more examples to drill addition with regrouping. By now, students should be quite comfortable with the skip counting for questions 2 and 3. You may want to provide coins to help them work out the answers for question 4.

Units 37 and 38 Subtraction

Materials
- tally chart
- tally cards
- about 40 popsicle sticks or strips of paper
- pieces of string

Objectives

Students should be able to:
- ✓ subtract a one- or two-digit number from a three-digit number with or without regrouping.

Suggested approach

Start with a word problem, for example:

- Joan has 184 mangoes. She sells 32 of them. How many mangoes are left?

Ask students how they might solve this problem. (By subtracting 32 from 184.) Demonstrate using the tally chart to solve the problem.

hundreds	tens	ones
1	8	4
	3	2
1	5	2

Remind the students how to do calculations like this. First, take away the ones.

$4 - 2 = 2$

Then take away the tens.

$8 - 3 = 5$

Unit-by-unit support 35

There are no hundreds to subtract.

Do a few more examples, and go through the example at the top of page 42 before asking the students to complete the questions in Unit 37.

The 'talk about' box on page 42 asks students to make up their own subtraction problems with hundreds, tens and ones for a partner to solve. They should then swap the problems back again so that they can be marked.

Students need to know how to regroup to be able to do the subtractions in Unit 38. Go through the examples on page 43 with the students. Explain that the same principle that they used in the previous unit applies here. So, for the first example:

First take away the ones.

We cannot take away 6 from 4 and so we need to change one ten into ten ones.

$14 - 6 = 8$

Then take away the tens.

Because we changed one ten into ten units, there are only eight tens left. However, we cannot take away 9 from 8 and so we need to change one hundred into a ten tens.

$18 - 9 = 9$

Now take away the hundreds.

Because we changed one hundred into ten tens, we have six hundreds left.

$6 - 2 = 4$

Do some more examples with the students, emphasising how we write the small numbers on the sum to remind us that we have regrouped. Once you are sure that the students are comfortable with this, ask them to do the questions in Unit 38.

Units 39 to 41 Measure

Materials
- metre rules
- tape measures
- string
- bottle caps, nails and balances
- various objects for weighing
- bag of sand or flour weighing 1 kilogram
- scale for measuring students' objects

Objectives

Students should be able to:

- ✓ select instruments and units of measurement
- ✓ differentiate between the use of centimetres and metres
- ✓ estimate and measure lengths, heights and distances
- ✓ measure perimeters of shapes
- ✓ explain why there is a need for centimetres
- ✓ compare, add and subtract linear measurements
- ✓ develop a sense of kilometres, grams and metres as units of measurement
- ✓ identify real-life situations where kg and g are used
- ✓ estimate, measure, compare and record mass in grams and kilograms
- ✓ compare the masses of different objects.

Suggested approach

Write the words 'height', 'length', 'width', 'breadth' and 'distance' on the board. Ask students what each word means. Explain that any line – whether it is straight or curved – has a length. Length is a measure of the distance along the line. Ask students what we mean by 'shorter' and 'longer'. They should realise that we can compare lines to see which is shorter and which is longer, but remind them that a line is only 'short' or 'long' in relation to other lines. The height of a door is longer than the height of a book, but much shorter than the length of a garden hose or a street.

When we describe the length of objects, we choose a side to measure. We use 'height' or 'length' to describe the longest or standing side of an object. 'Breadth' or 'width' is used to describe the distance across the object from one side to the other.

Ask: What units do we use to measure length? (Millimetres, centimetres, metres, kilometres.) Give examples of different lengths and ask students which units they would use to measure the lengths (for example, the distance between two cities, the length of a whale, the length of a boat, the length of a fingernail, and so on).

Ask: What instrument could I use to measure the height of the board? (A ruler or tape measure.) Use a ruler or tape measure and ask one of the students to come and read the measurement. Students should already know how to read metric units off a measuring tape. If necessary, demonstrate how to read the calibrations. You may also wish to write the abbreviations (m, cm, mm) on the board.

Give out metre rules or tape measures. Get students to work in groups on activity 1 in Unit 39. Get students to explain the concept of perimeter before they complete question 2 in Unit 39.

Unit-by-unit support

For Unit 40, show the class two similar-sized objects. Ask them to tell you which object they think is heavier. Ask two or three students to lift up the objects. Ask: Which do you think is heavier now? Finally, put the objects on a balance to check whether the answers were correct. Remind students that the side of the balance that goes down has the heavier object.

Show the class how to find the mass of an object, using bottle caps. Put a pencil in one balance pan. Ask the class how many bottle caps they will need to balance the pencil. Put the bottle caps in the other pan, one by one, until the pans balance.

Ask students whether they know the units we use to measure mass. Show them the 1 kg bag of flour or sand and let students take turns picking up the bag to get a sense of what its mass is. Explain that 1 kg equals 1 000 g. Items that are lighter than a kilogram are measured in grams. Get students to work through Unit 40 in their Pupil Books.

Divide the students into groups. Give each group an object. Ask them to decide whether the object's mass is more than, less than, or about 1 kg. They can write more specific answers into the table in Unit 41 in their Pupil Books. Then let them work individually through question 2 in Unit 41.

Unit 42 Temperature

Materials
- a range of thermometers
- ice
- kettle
- water

Objectives

Students should be able to:
- name instruments used to measure temperature
- work with units used to measure temperature
- describe recorded temperatures using phrases such as 'warm', 'very hot', etc
- recognise standard temperature readings such as freezing point, body temperature, and so on.

Suggested approach

Have a discussion with the students about hot and cold. Talk about the weather, about the hottest and coldest things students can think of. Encourage students to talk comparatively about hot and cold. For example, a cup of tea is hot, but the sun is far hotter; rain is cold, but ice is colder, and so on. Emphasise that temperature is relative: ice is colder than rain; food in a refrigerator is warmer than food in a freezer, and so on.

Display the thermometers. You should have an oral thermometer, a food thermometer and a room thermometer. Discuss how and when each thermometer is used. A room thermometer can be used continuously to measure the temperature, whereas an oral thermometer is usually used when someone feels sick or feverish. We also use thermometers in refrigerators, freezers and other cold storage areas, in order to check that the temperature is kept low enough to prevent food from spoiling.

Divide the students into groups. Each group may then find the appropriate thermometer to find the temperature of each of the following:
- boiling water
- ice
- room temperature
- cold water
- tap water
- body temperature.

Turn to Pupil Book Unit 42. Read through question 1, and discuss the students' responses orally. Then ask students what they can see in each of the photographs. Let the students read the sentence below each photograph. Then ask them questions to encourage them to memorise these standard temperatures. Let them complete questions 2 and 3, then go through the answers.

Unit 43 Subtraction

Objectives
Students should be able to:
- ✓ subtract a two-digit number from a three-digit number with or without regrouping.

Suggested approach

In this unit, students are given more practice at subtraction with regrouping. Students learnt how to do this in Units 37 and 38. Use the guidelines for teaching this concept on pages 35–36 of this Teacher's Guide if you think students need more practice before they attempt the unit.

Go through the worked example at the top of page 48 with the students. Repeat with more examples of your own if you think it is necessary. Then let students complete the questions in Unit 43.

Units 44 and 45 Time

Materials
- large teacher-made clock
- real clock
- small clock for each student
- clock face stamp

Objectives
Students should be able to:
- ✓ associate events with specific times
- ✓ use time vocabulary appropriately
- ✓ write the correct notation for times on the hour, half hour, quarter hour.

Suggested approach

Quickly review time on the hour, half hour and quarter hour, as covered in Units 23 and 24.

Unit-by-unit support   39

Set your large clock to 12:15. Allow the students to tell the time. Some students may know the time as quarter past 12. If they are not familiar with this time, introduce it. Repeat with several examples involving quarter past the hour. Let the students show the times on their individual clocks. Also demonstrate the time on the real clock so that students can see the exact position of the hands (the small hand does not point exactly to the hour number, because it is already a quarter of the way closer to the next hour).

Explain that when the hour has not arrived, we can count the time before the hour. Set your large clock to quarter to 12. Let the students suggest the time. Discuss the time, using the real clock to show the exact position of the hands.

Repeat with several examples to illustrate quarter to the hour. Let the students use their clocks to show each of the times discussed. Let students work through Unit 44 in their Pupil Books.

Display your large clock. Talk about the marks around the edge of the clock as minute marks. Ask the students to guess the number of minute marks, or allow them to count the minute marks. Explain that each mark represents one minute, and that the 60 marks represent 60 minutes, which is one hour.

Use the real clock to show 1 o'clock. Let the students tell the time. Turn the back knob slowly so that the students can watch the hands move. Stop the clock at 2 o'clock. Ask the students to tell the time duration from 1 o'clock to 2 o'clock. (One hour.) Ask the students to tell you the number of minutes in one hour (60.) Emphasise that 60 minutes makes one hour. Explain that as the long hand moves around the clock from one number to the next, we add five more minutes past the hour.

Ask students to set their clocks to 3 o'clock. Then ask them to show quarter past 3. Ask them to count the minutes to tell exactly how many minutes past 3. Help them to count the minutes. Show the different ways of writing this time: quarter past 3; fifteen minutes past 3; 3:15. Then repeat this procedure to show half past the hour. Show the notation and expressions: 4:30; half past 4; thirty minutes past 4.

CD-Rom activity
- Time

Let students work through Unit 45.

Units 46 and 47 Fractions

Materials
- circular and rectangular cut-outs
- bottle caps or stone

Objectives

Students should be able to:
- work with fractions.

Suggested approach

For these units, follow the same procedure as for Units 21 and 22. Hand out the paper cut-outs and get students to demonstrate different fractions. Note that it will be easier to use long rectangles for fractions with odd denominators ($\frac{1}{5}$, $\frac{1}{3}$, and so on). Students can use circular cut-outs for demonstrating fractions with even denominators ($\frac{1}{4}$, $\frac{1}{6}$, and so on).

Similarly, set out large groups of bottle caps or stones and get students to set aside fractions of the set, for example $\frac{1}{4}$ of 32, $\frac{1}{7}$ of 21, and so on.

Then let students work through Units 46 and 47 in their Pupil Books.

Unit 48 Tables and graphs

Materials
- scale for measuring students' masses

Objectives

Students should be able to:
- ✓ measure mass
- ✓ collect data through observation, interviews
- ✓ read and interpret information from a bar graph
- ✓ use tally charts, tables and graphs.

Suggested approach

Revise the word 'kilogram'. Read through the questions in Unit 48, and make sure students understand the concepts of 'scale', 'axis' (vertical and horizontal), and that they know how to lay out a bar or block graph. Let students work in groups to measure each other's mass and answer the questions in Unit 48.

Additional activities
Probability

Teachers in Jamaica need to include some work on probability. Write the words 'probability', 'chance', 'likely' and 'unlikely'. Ask students if they know what these words mean, and let the students help you to develop some definitions. Show the students a coin. Explain the phrase 'possible outcome' by asking what the possible outcomes are of flipping the coin. There are two possible outcomes – landing on heads, and landing on tails. Tell them that you are going to flip the coin ten times, and ask how many times out of ten they think the coin will land on heads. Have a class discussion about probability – the likelihood that something will happen – and encourage the students to work out that the probability is that the coin should land about five times on heads. Draw a tally chart on the board with the headings 'Heads' and 'Tails'. Call one student up to mark the tallies in the correct place each time you flip the coin. Flip ten times, and mark a tally in the correct box each time. Repeat the experiment a few times. Then let students work in pairs to do a similar experiment using dice. They should first identify the possible outcomes, then predict the probable outcomes. As they conduct their experiments, they should mark the outcomes in tally charts; they will need six tally columns for each of the possible outcomes. They should then compare their outcomes with their predicted outcomes.

Units 49 and 50 Assessment

> **Objectives**
>
> Students should be able to:
> - calculate the total cost of a set of items
> - subtract a two-digit number from a three-digit number with or without regrouping
> - make amounts of money using various combinations of coins
> - write correct time notations
> - work with fractions
> - solve real-life problems involving mass and height.

Suggested approach

Units 49 and 50 can be used to revise and assess material covered in Units 37 to 48. You can use Unit 49 as a class test. Question 1 presents real-life questions involving money, but actually tests addition of two-digit numbers with and without regrouping. Make sure that students understand that they should find the total cost of each pair of items. You may want to make up a different example in order to remind students how to regroup using a tally chart. By now, they should be able to solve questions involving money without using actual coins to help them.

Question 2 deals with subtraction with and without re-grouping. Question 3 deals with skip counting. By now, students should be adept at both of these skills. For question 4, you may want to provide some pretend coins in order to remind students of the denominations of coins to use in their answers. More advanced students should not require this practical support.

Unit 50 gives students work on real-life problems involving length and mass. Questions 1 to 3 can be done for homework. Students should go with a parent or guardian to the supermarket, or, if you have time, you may want to arrange a class outing to a nearby shop. Question 4 assesses students' ability to read and represent time. They can work individually on this question.

Units 51 to 55 — Shape and space

Materials
- cut-outs of plane shapes (circles, stars, triangles, squares, rectangles, pentagons, etc.)
- dice
- matchboxes
- empty tins
- balls
- cone-shaped party hats
- drawings of solid shapes
- examples of solids with different numbers of faces (prisms, pyramids, cuboids)
- stiff card or paper
- sticky tape

Objectives
Students should be able to:
- ✓ identify and name points, lines, rays, angles and right angles
- ✓ identify angles that are equal to, greater than, and smaller than a right angle
- ✓ identify, draw and construct cubes, cuboids, cylinders, cones, spheres
- ✓ count and describe the sides and angles of plane shapes
- ✓ use a ruler to draw and measure lines
- ✓ identify solids in the environment and describe their uses
- ✓ describe differences and similarities between shapes in the environment
- ✓ identify similarities between cubes and cuboids, and between cones and cylinders
- ✓ identify parts of three-dimensional shapes: faces, edges and vertices.

Suggested approach

Write the following words on the board: point, line, angle. Ask students if they can explain the meanings of each word. Let them illustrate their definitions by drawing points, lines and angles on the board. A point is represented as a dot. The corner of a shape is the point where the sides intersect. A line is the shortest distance between two points. An angle is formed when two lines meet. Give different students opportunities to draw points, lines and angles on the board. Show them how to label and name their points, lines and angles using capital letters, for example, line AB.

Then ask students to describe a right angle. Use a rectangular sheet of paper to demonstrate: fold the paper in half, then fold it in half again. The first fold makes a straight line or an angle of 180°. The second fold divides the line in half, making 90°.

Ask students to look at the picture in Unit 51. Ask them to identify shapes in the picture. They should be able to find squares, a star, rectangles, circles, a triangle and a hexagon. You may want to point out the difference between the shapes of the books in the picture and the shape of a real book; in the picture, the rectangles are distorted to show perspective. Get students to count the number of sides and angles in each shape they identify.

Students can complete Unit 51 in their Pupil Books. Again, get them to count the numbers of sides and angles in each shape.

Additional activities

Constructing and measuring lines, angles and shapes

As an additional exercise, get students to use a ruler to draw and measure lines in their books. They can then check each other's work by measuring a partner's drawn lines. You can also get students to construct lines, angles and shapes. Here are some examples of these types of activities.

1. Draw a square ABCD whose sides each measure 5 cm.
2. Draw a triangle WXY whose longest side, WX, measures 8 cm.
3. Draw a rectangle with two sides, PQ and RS, that each measure 4 cm and two sides, PS and RQ, that each measure 3 cm.
4. Use paper to make a right angle. Use your paper angle to help you to draw a right angle. Label your angle EFG.
5. Draw three different triangles. All the triangles must have one side that measures 5 cm, but the other two sides should be different lengths.

Draw a right angle on the board. Then draw two more angles on the board: one greater than a right and angle and one less than a right angle. Try to make sure that the lengths of the arms are the same. Point to the right angle and ask the students what we call this angle. Now point to one of the other angles and ask them whether it is less than or greater than a right angle. Repeat with the other angle.

Ask a student to come to the board and draw another angle that is less than a right angle. Ask another student to draw an angle that is greater than a right angle. Repeat a few more times before asking the students to complete the questions in Unit 52. In question 2, students have to write down the letters of the angles that fit each of the descriptions.

Unit 53 deals with solids. Display the different examples of solids on a table. Go through the information in Unit 53 together with the class.

Divide the students into groups of three and four, and give each group a ball. Question the students about the shape of the ball. (Round.) Tell the students that this shape is called a sphere.

Pin a drawing of a sphere to the board. Write the word 'sphere' on the board. Ask the students to tell you the names of other objects that are the same shape, such as a marble, basketball, netball, and so on. Ask students to explain why it is important for a ball to be a sphere and not some other shape. (A ball needs to bounce, roll, and so on; shapes with corners do not roll.)

Give each group a die and ask the students to look at it closely. Question them about the number of sides (six) and the size of each side (all the sides are the same size). Tell the students that this shape is called a cube. Pin a drawing of a cube to the board, and write the word 'cube'. Again, ask them to explain why the shape is important or useful. Ask the students to name some other objects that are cube-shaped. Then repeat this procedure, but use a matchbox (cuboid). Do the same with a tin (cylinder) and party hat (cone). Cuboids include: books, boxes for various products (washing powder, sweets, pasta, and so on), cupboards and so on. Cylinders include: tubes, pipes, some buildings. Cones include: traffic cones, ice-cream cones, party hats, packaging for certain kinds of sweets.

Let students work through Unit 53. Then let students work through Unit 54. They can use the pictures in Unit 53 to help them.

Additional activities
Similarities and differences between solids
1 Ask students to describe the similarities between cubes and cuboids. They should realise that both solids have six flat sides, eight corners and twelve straight edges. However, a cube has six square faces, all identical in size, whilst a cuboid has at least four rectangular sides.
2 Get students to identify similarities and differences between cones and cylinders. They should realise that both cones and cylinders have flat circular faces. However, a cone has only one flat circular face, and a curved face that tapers up to a point. A cylinder has two flat circular faces, and a curved rectangular face.
3 Students should construct solid shapes using a variety of materials – card and tape, or paper and string, or clay. Provide the materials and give students specific shapes to construct, including cubes, spheres, cylinders, cones and cuboids.

Ask students if they know what a face is. They may point to their own faces. Ask what else we describe as a face (the flat side of a solid). If necessary, demonstrate by showing a solid shape and pointing out the faces. Pick up different solids and ask students to count the faces of each solid. Then ask them to count the edges. If necessary, explain that the edges are the lines where two faces meet. Hand out stiff paper or card and sticky tape so that students can make models of the solid shapes. More advanced students can cut out their own sides for their shapes, but you may want to have some examples prepared in order to show them how to make the shapes. Then let students work through Unit 55.

Units 56 to 60 Number operations

Materials
- bottle caps or small stones
- domino cards with multiplication sums on them

Objectives
Students should be able to:
- ✓ recall basic facts of addition and subtraction
- ✓ add and subtract whole numbers to three digits, with and without regrouping
- ✓ multiply two-digit numbers by one-digit numbers
- ✓ understand multiplication as repeated addition
- ✓ use division to check multiplication answers
- ✓ work with expanded notation.

Suggested approach

In Unit 56, students review addition and subtraction, as well as word sums which involve these two operations. Students should be able to add and subtract numbers with up to three digits, with and without regrouping.

Write the following example on the board: 42 + 23.

As you write the problem in columns, ask the students to explain how many tens and units are in each number. Let a student come to the board and solve it. Then write the following on the board: 242 + 23.

Ask the students what is different about this sum (the first number is now a three-digit number, which has two hundreds as well as four tens and two units). Work through the example, emphasising the importance of lining up the ones, tens and hundreds. Work through some different examples, such as: 102 + 45, 533 + 22.

Students can now practise adding two-digit and three-digit numbers without regrouping. Here are some examples you can use:

a 217 + 22   **b** 431 + 64   **c** 911 + 35
d 43 + 102   **e** 21 + 913   **f** 365 + 34
g 700 + 65   **h** 941 + 13

Next, work through an example of adding a two-digit and a three-digit number with regrouping, for example: 157 + 23, 239 + 42, 479 + 43.

As you go through the third example, explain that we regroup hundreds in the same way as we regroup ones and tens. Give students some practice in adding three-digit numbers and two-digit numbers with regrouping.

Follow a similar procedure for subtractions up to three digits. Write the following example on the board: 29 – 17.

Ask students to identify the tens and ones in each number. Write the problem in columns, and let a student come to the board and solve it. Then write the following on the board: 129 – 17.

Again, write the problem in columns, emphasising the importance of lining up from the right-hand side – ones, tens, hundreds. Give a few more examples of subtraction without regrouping for students to solve.

Then move on to subtraction with regrouping. Write up the following example on the board, and explain each step as you regroup in order to subtract: 325 – 46.

Do a few more examples with the class, then give them some examples to solve on their own. Students can then do the questions in Unit 56.

Additional activities
Subtracting numbers with up to four digits
In St Lucian schools, students need to add and subtract numbers with up to four digits. Teachers should demonstrate appropriate examples and can use the following examples for drilling:

a 440 + 200   **b** 640 + 135   **c** 780 + 119
d 157 + 235   **e** 768 + 27   **f** 974 + 135
g 2 132 + 1 225   **h** 6 450 + 2 327   **i** 4 242 + 3 415
j 235 + 5 678   **k** 995 + 1 230   **l** 788 + 2 350
m 648 + 1 372   **n** 2 475 + 1 289

> ### Addition with up to six-digit numbers
> In Jamaican schools, students need to add numbers with up to six digits. Teachers can use the following examples for drilling. Note that students should get used to adding more than two numbers in a sum. Emphasise that they should line up the ones, tens, hundreds, thousands, and so on.
>
> 1. a 4 500 + 2 999
>   c 2 335 + 2 487
>   e 199 + 2 085
>   g 3 005 + 1 119
>   b 1 278 + 4 311
>   d 6 450 + 1 275
>   f 5 678 + 278
>   h 4 325 + 1 023
>
> 2. a 450 + 450 + 1299
>   c 865 + 1 250 + 6 342
>   b 230 + 1 495 + 1 108
>
> 3. a 546 125 + 124 011
>   c 99 + 20 189
>   b 10 450 + 175
>   d 155 + 2 450 + 23 699
>
> 4. a 378 + 295 + 1 209 + 102
>   c 155 + 806 + 3 976 + 23
>   b 138 + 899 + 12 650 + 3 455
>   d 250 + 735 + 1 144 + 18 065
>
> Teachers should also make up their own examples for drilling. Note that property prices, population sizes and travel distances all make good examples for exercises involving large numbers.

Unit 57 involves students writing out numbers to 999 in figures and in words. On the board, write the figures 100, 200, 300 to 900 in a list. Next to each one, write the numbers in words.

Then write, for example, 347 on the board. Ask a student what number this is. (Three hundred and forty-seven.) Ask them how they would write this number in words. Ask the student to come and write it on the board.

Repeat with more examples before asking the students to complete the questions in Unit 57.

Unit 58 deals with multiplication. Read through the example at the top of page 63 in the Pupil Book. You may wish to use stones or bottle caps to demonstrate practically. Ask the following questions about the example: How many cookies are on one plate? How many cookies are on two plates? What are the different number sentences we could write to describe this problem? (4 + 4 = 8 or 4 × 2 = 8.)

Let the students use the stones or bottle tops to work practically through the questions in Unit 58 in their Pupil Books. Students should work through Unit 59 without using objects. However, they can draw sets in order to help them work out the answers.

To begin Unit 60, introduce multiplication of two-digit numbers. Start with multiplication by one. First, orally get the students to multiply one-digit numbers by one, for example: 2 × 1, 4 × 1, 8 × 1, and so on.

Start asking them to multiply two-digit numbers by one, for example: 12 × 1, 17 × 1, 28 × 1, and so on. Then introduce multiplication by two. Write the following example on the board: 13 × 2.

$$\begin{array}{r} 13 \\ \times\ 2 \\ \hline = 26 \end{array}$$

Write the problem in columns and show the students how to work it out using tens and ones.

Go through a few more examples using different one-digit numbers, for example: 24 × 2, 21 × 4, 30 × 3.

Then write the following example on the board: 53 × 6.

$$\begin{array}{r} 53 \\ \times\ 6 \\ \hline = 318 \end{array}$$

Write the problem in columns and demonstrate how to work out the answer by carrying the extra ten produced in the ones column over to the tens column. Emphasise that we add the extra ten produced in the ones column to the product of the tens column.

Go through a few more examples, such as: 63 × 5, 42 × 7, 23 × 9 and so on. Then let students work through some examples on their own.

Go through the example in Unit 60 with the students, demonstrating how they can use columns to help them multiply bigger numbers. The let them work through the questions on page 65.

Unit 61 Review

Objectives

Students should be able to:
- identify shapes and angles
- use operations to solve word sums.

Suggested approach

Let students work individually on Unit 61. Some examples they should notice include: spheres (ball, balloons, scoops of ice-cream), cones (ice-cream cones), cylinders (litter cans, binoculars, cans of cola), cubes (popcorn boxes), cuboids (vendors' boxes, camera, stadium platforms). There are also a variety of right angles in the picture, most noticeably the corners of each level in the stands. Make sure that the students do not mistake the circular lollipop for a sphere; similarly they should not mistake the rectangular banners for cuboids.

Units 62 and 63   Rounding off

Materials
- number line with multiples of ten marked in bold

Objectives
Students should be able to:
- ✓ round off two-digit numbers to the nearest ten
- ✓ use rounding off to estimate for addition and subtraction
- ✓ round off three-digit numbers to the nearest ten.

Suggested approach

Ask a student to point out where ten lies on the number line. Do the same for 20, 30, 40, and so on up to 100. Then ask a student to mark where three lies on the number line. Ask: Is it closer to zero or to ten? (It is closer to ten.) Then do the same for the following numbers: 12, 9, 4, 6. Explain that we can round off numbers to the nearest ten in order to give an approximate amount. If the units equal five or more, we round the number up to ten, or to the next ten. If the units equal less than five, we round the number down to 0. Ask students to round numbers off to the nearest ten, working orally, and get them to demonstrate on the number line. Students can practise rounding off various numbers. Use question 1 from the **Additional activities** below to give students some practice in rounding off. Let students complete Units 62 and 63.

Point out that sometimes we use rounding off to estimate for addition and subtraction. Give students the following example:
- I have 52 red sweets and 79 green sweets. Approximately how many do I have altogether?

CD-Rom activity
- Rounding off

Get the students to round off 52 to 50, and 79 to 80. Then they can easily add the tens. Use questions 2 and 3 from the **Additional activities** below to give students some practice in rounding off to estimate for addition and subtraction.

Additional activities

Rounding off two-digit numbers
1 Round off the following numbers to the nearest ten.
   a 8   b 12   c 15   d 19   e 11
   f 25   g 94   h 99   i 16   j 83
2 Round off to solve each word sum. Give the approximate answer each time. Then find the accurate answer and work out the difference between the approximate answer and the accurate answer.
   a Janet has 33 red buttons, 78 blue buttons and 45 pink buttons. Approximately how many buttons does she have altogether?
   b There were guests from four different countries staying at a hotel. 27 guests were from South Africa, 39 guests were from Japan, 22 guests were from Italy and 11 guests were from Australia. Approximately how many guests were there altogether?
   c The school librarian ordered some new books. She ordered 53 storybooks, 12 picture books, 19 science books, 2 atlases and 22 reference books. Approximately how many books did she order altogether?

Unit-by-unit support

3 Round off to solve each word sum. Give the approximate answer each time. Then find the accurate answer and work out the difference between the approximate answer and the accurate answer.

   a 152 children went on a school outing. 129 children were wearing sunhats during the outing. Approximately how many children did not wear sunhats?

   b Mrs Bloom had 44 roses in her garden. She picked 17 roses. Approximately how many roses did she have left in the garden?

   c Molly made 96 cookies. She took 52 cookies to school. Approximately how many cookies did she not take to school?

Rounding off three-digit numbers

Students in OECS territories need to round off three-digit numbers to the nearest ten or 100. Teachers in these areas should work through some examples, then give students the following examples for drilling:

1 Round off to the nearest ten.

   a 343   **b** 105   **c** 987   **d** 498   **e** 111
   f 545   **g** 102   **h** 249   **i** 859   **j** 899

2 Round off to the nearest 100.

   a 855   **b** 150   **c** 199   **d** 249   **e** 738
   f 109   **g** 277   **h** 566   **i** 136   **j** 462

Units 64 and 65   Capacity

Materials
- cups
- jars
- bottles
- funnels
- jugs
- large bucket of water or tap

Objectives

Students should be able to:
- ✓ estimate and measure capacity of containers
- ✓ use litres, millilitres and centilitres for measuring capacity
- ✓ describe real-life uses for measuring capacity.

Suggested approach

Hold up two containers of similar size. Ask: Which container do you think holds more? How could you check? (By filling one container and using it to fill the other.) Demonstrate carefully, using a funnel if necessary. Emphasise that we must be careful when working with water, and should not overfill containers.

Put the students into groups of four. Ask them to fill in their guesses about the containers in Unit 64. Then distribute the containers; each group should have a funnel for decanting water from one container to the next. Some teachers may prefer to take their class outside for this activity. Let students fill each container – from either the bucket or the tap – and then write their results for which container held the most, least and so on.

Show the class how to find the capacity of a bottle using cups as a unit of measurement. Emphasise that the cup must be filled with water to the same level each time. Let students guess how many cupfuls are needed first. Then give each group four bottles. They should label the bottles A, B, C and D. Each group should fill in the first column of the table in Unit 64. Let the groups measure the capacity of each bottle, using cups. Then they should complete Units 64 and 65. For activity 3 in Unit 65, students will need a bucket, a small cup and a large cup for each pair of students. Again, some teachers may prefer to take students outside for this activity.

Explain that the standard unit of capacity is the litre. Introduce the units of capacity by writing the units of capacity and their abbreviations on the board:

millilitres – ml; centilitres – cl; litres – l; kilolitres – kl

Ask students to guess how many millilitres make up a litre. (1 000.) Write on the board: 1 000 ml = 1 l

Then ask them to guess how many centilitres make up a litre. (100.) Write on the board: 100 cl = 1 l

Then ask them to guess how many litres make up a kilolitre (1 000). Write on the board: 1 000 l = 1 kl

Ask students to give examples of products that they know are measured in millilitres. Examples could include: nail varnish, perfume, small containers of juice and other drinks, medicines, shampoo, and any other liquid products sold in containers smaller than a litre. Then ask students to give examples of products sold in litres. Examples could include: paint, large tins of oil, gasoline and diesel, and so on. Let students complete the additional activities below.

Additional activities

1 Draw pictures of three things that are usually measured in millilitres.
2 Say whether you would measure each of the following in litres or millilitres.
   a Juice for 20 children   **b** One glass of juice   **c** Paint to cover a whole house
3 **a** How many millilitres make up one litre?
   b How many centilitres make up one litre?

Note that OECS students need to discuss why we need to use centilitres. OECS teachers can have a class discussion about this.

Units 66 to 68 Date and time

Materials
- calendar with local public holidays
- large teacher-made clocks

Objectives

Students should be able to:
- ✓ state and write dates in a variety of ways
- ✓ state the relationship between units of time, including hours and minutes, years and months, weeks and days
- ✓ create and solve problems using time.

Suggested approach

Show students the calendar. Ask them why they think we use calendars. Open the calendar to the current month. Ask the following kinds of questions:
- What month are we in now?
- How many days does this month have?
- What day did the first of the month fall on?
- How many Sundays are there in this month?
- What day will the next month start on?
- What day did the last month end on?

Get students to identify days given by you, such as: the first day of the month, the fifteenth day of the month, the twenty-second day of the month, and so on.

Ask students to say the name of the first month in a year. Someone should suggest January; get that student to write the month name on the board. Continue in the same way for all the months. Get the students to read through the names of the twelve months in order. Ask some volunteers to recite the months of the year with their eyes closed, or with their back to the board.

Ask students to name the different units we use to measure time. If necessary, elicit the following answers: seconds, days, minutes, hours, weeks, months, years. Write these terms on the board. Ask students to put the units in order from the shortest unit of time to the longest unit of time. Orally quiz the students using the following kinds of questions:
- How many seconds are there in a minute?
- How many minutes are there in an hour?
- How many hours are there in a day?
- How many days are there in a week?
- How many weeks are there in a year?
- How many months are there in a year?

Introduce ways of writing the date. Write the date on the board using the following convention: 22 January 2003. Say that we could also express this as the twenty-second day of the first month in 2003. Explain that we can also represent dates using only numbers. There are two ways of doing this: day, then month, then year or year, then month, then day. Some variations include:

22/01/2003, 2003/01/22; 22-01-2003, 2003-01-22.

Explain that sometimes we abbreviate the names of months by using the first three letters, for example Sep instead of September, or Mar instead of March. The only month name that does not get abbreviated is May. Get students to say and write dates in different ways.

They can then do the questions in Unit 66.

Units 67 and 68 deal with duration. Go through the example in Unit 67. Demonstrate, using your large clock, the passing of two hours. Move the hands of the clock to various times on the hour and get students to say what the time is. Let students complete the questions in Unit 67.

Move the clock hands to show five o'clock. Ask students how they could write this time. (5:00.) Let a student demonstrate writing the time. Say that you want them to show that it is five o'clock in the afternoon. If necessary, remind them that we write pm for afternoon and evening times (times after midday and before midnight) and am for morning times (times after midnight and before midday). Show some different times on the clock face, and let different students demonstrate how to write the time. Then let students work through Unit 68.

The 'talk about' box in Unit 68 invites students to talk about their daily activities, and how much time these take. Expect suggestions such as eating breakfast, getting dressed, bathing, tying shoelaces, making the bed, doing homework, and so on. Going to school probably takes up the most time, followed by after-school activities such as sports and games. However, different students will have different answers.

Students also need to create their own problems about time. Make sure the time vocabulary is still on the board, or write it up again: day, second, hour, minute, week, month, year. Ask students each to make up five problems using the time vocabulary. Then they can exchange time problems, solve them, then exchange again for checking.

Unit 69 Operations game

Objectives

Students should be able to:

- add and subtract with and without regrouping.

Suggested approach

You can use Unit 69 as a fun revision exercise for the students. Go over addition and subtraction with and without regrouping if you think that it is necessary. Explain to the students that once they have worked out the problems, they have to shade in the correct answer in the grid. If all their answers are correct, they should see a letter of the alphabet.

Units 70 and 71 Assessment

Objectives

Students should be able to:
- ✓ identify and name solid shapes
- ✓ solve word problems involving multiplication
- ✓ compare capacities of different containers
- ✓ round off to the nearest ten
- ✓ work with calendars
- ✓ write dates
- ✓ subtract with regrouping.

Suggested approach

Use Units 70 and 71 as class tests to assess the skills covered in Units 51 to 69.

Units 72 and 73 Measure

Materials
- long rulers
- tape measures

Objectives

Students should be able to:
- ✓ use the terms metre and centimetre
- ✓ estimate, measure and compare lengths in metres and centimetres
- ✓ differentiate between kilometres, metres and centimetres
- ✓ collect and record data
- ✓ compare results
- ✓ explain the advantages of representing data in tables and graphs
- ✓ estimate and measure area using square centimetres
- ✓ create and solve problems using linear measurements.

Suggested approach

Ask students if they remember the units we use to measure length. They should suggest centimetres, millimetres, metres and kilometres. Write each word on the board, with its abbreviation, as follows:

millimetre – mm; centimetre – cm; metre – m; kilometre – km

Ask: How many millimetres make up a centimetre? (Ten.) How many centimetres make up a metre? (100.) How many metres make up a kilometre? (1 000.)

Students have already measured each other's heights. This time, they should measure each other's heights and compare the results to their previous results. This activity combines measuring skills with data-handling skills. Let students work in pairs to measure each other's heights. Then they should collect the results from other pairs, record it in their tables and work out whether each student has grown.

The 'talk about' box in Unit 72 invites students to discuss the uses of tables and graphs. Students should realise that tables help us to list and compare information in a clear, easy-to-read way. A graph can also show how something changes; for example, if a child measures her height every six months, and makes a graph from the results, she will be able to see how quickly she is growing.

Make up some word problems, for example: Mary is 133 cm tall and her younger sister is 58 cm tall. What is their total height? Give these to the students to do on their own, or you can complete them as a class.

Then ask the students to make up some number problems of their own. These problems should involve addition and subtraction. Students give their problems to a partner to complete. When finished, students should swap the problems back again to be marked.

Ask students to complete the word problems in Unit 73. You may need to read through the problems with the students before they begin.

Additional activities
Working with square centimetres

Students in Trinidad and Jamaica are required to estimate and measure surface area using square centimetres. You can introduce the concept of area using centimetre square paper. Introduce the concept of a square centimetre, and demonstrate how to find the areas of simple plane shapes. At this stage, students do not need to work with formulae; they just need to work with square centimetres on grid paper. Get students to draw shapes of given sizes and to work out the area by counting square centimetres.

Unit 74 Money

Materials
- pretend money
- $5, $10, $20 and $50 notes
- newspapers with advertisements for department stores, clothing stores and food stores

Objectives

Students should be able to:
- describe the $5, $10, $20 and $50 notes
- calculate the total cost of a set of items
- calculate change
- approximate to the nearest $1, $10 or $100
- read and write money amounts to $999.99 using the $ symbol and decimal point
- round off answers to the nearest $1, $10, $100.

Suggested approach

Show the students the $5, $10, $20 and $50 notes. Ask the students to describe each of the notes, emphasising the differences between the notes. Ask the students how they would recognise each note.

Show the class the newspaper advertisements and ask them to read out prices of specific items. Go through the examples at the top of page 79 in the Pupil Book, getting students to read out the prices. Ask questions such as:

- What is the most expensive item?
- What is the cheapest item?
- If I had a $10 note, which item could I buy? How much change would I have?

Let students work through the questions in Unit 74.

CD-Rom activity
- Money

Additional activities
Working with money
1. Write the following using the $ symbol and decimal point.
   a. fifty-five dollars and seventy-seven cents
   b. two hundred and fifty-three dollars and nineteen cents
   c. nine hundred and forty-four dollars and sixty-eight cents
   d. eight hundred and sixteen dollars and sixty cents
2. Work out each total, then round off to the nearest $1.
   a. $7.70 + $8.35 + $12.59   b. $5.20 + $9.35 + $15.72
   c. $9.99 + $10.39 + $16.97
3. Work out each total, then round off to the nearest $10.
   a. $59.90 + $65.49 + $19.25   b. $13.33 + $74.69 + $26.90
   c. $120.55 + $38.59 + $27.44
4. Work out each total, then round off to the nearest $100.
   a. $155.68 + $132.24 + $365.98   b. $221.50 + $315.65 + $110.05
   c. $100.32 + $119.99 + $165.79

Unit 75 Multiplying by 1 and 0

Materials
- bottle caps

Objectives
Students should be able to:
- multiply by 1 and 0.

Suggested approach

Write the following number sentence on the board: $2 \times 0 = $ ___.

Then ask the students to use their bottle caps to find the answer. Let one student try to complete the number sentence on the board by drawing the appropriate sets.

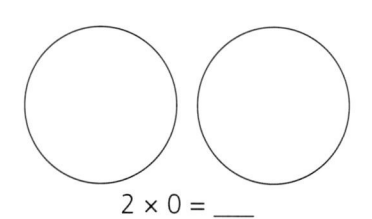

$2 \times 0 = $ ___

Ask: How many sets? (Two.) How many objects in each set? (Zero.) How many objects altogether? (Zero.) $2 \times 0 = 0$. Do not erase this example yet. Do some other examples in the same way. Leave all the examples on the board. Draw the students' attention to the number sentences. Question them about the answers obtained for the different number sentences. Help them realise that any number multiplied by 0 equals 0.

Write the following number sentence on the board: $2 \times 1 = $ ___.

Let a student draw sets of objects and complete the number sentence 2 × 1 = 2. Do not erase this example. Do other examples, such as 4 × 1, 5 × 1, 8 × 1. Leave all the examples on the board. Ask the students to look at the examples. Question them about the answers obtained for different number sentences. Help them to realise that when any number is multiplied by 1, the result is the original number. Then let students complete Unit 75.

Units 76 and 77   Pictographs

Materials
- pictograph as shown

Objectives

Students should be able to:
- ✓ read information from pictographs
- ✓ explain why it may be necessary to use one picture or block to represent more than one unit of data.

Suggested approach

Turn to page 81. The 'talk about' box in Unit 76 asks the students to think about how they could show large numbers on a pictograph. You could give them a hint by drawing a simple pictograph on the board that shows lots of numbers for each category. Help the students to see that if one picture were worth, for example two units, then the pictograph would be much easier to read and to draw.

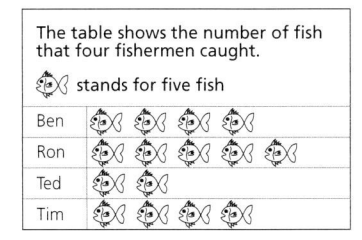

Draw a stick man on the board. Tell the class that the stick man represents two boys. Draw another stick man. Ask: How many boys do these two stick men represent? (Four boys.) Draw a third stick man. Ask: How many boys now? (Six.) Repeat for a fourth and fifth stick man.

Draw a fish on the board. Say that the fish represents five fish. Ask a student to come up and draw a picture that represents ten fish. Repeat for other amounts of fish.

Tell the students to look at the pictograph in Unit 76. Ask: What does each picture stand for? (Three ice creams.) How many ice creams were sold on Friday? (12 ice creams.) And so on. Then let students complete Unit 76.

Review the questions and answers of Unit 76 before going on to Unit 77. Display the pictograph showing how many eggs that five girls ate in two weeks. Encourage students to pose questions about the pictograph and let other students give answers.

Let the students complete Unit 77 on their own.

CD-Rom activity
- Pictographs

Unit-by-unit support 57

Units 78 and 79 — Bar graphs

Objectives

Students should be able to:

- ✓ describe how to collect data using observation and interviewing
- ✓ explain when it is appropriate to use observation and interviews to collect data
- ✓ create problems that may be answered through data collection, representation and interpretation
- ✓ plan for data collection activities
- ✓ collect sets of data through observation and interviews to answer questions of interest
- ✓ select an appropriate method (pictograph or bar graph) and scale to represent a set of collected data.

Suggested approach

Explain to the students that in the same way that we can use one picture to represent more than one unit of data in a pictograph, we can use one block in a bar graph to represent more than one unit of data.

Turn to Unit 78 and look at the bar graph at the top of page 83 with the students. Ask the students questions about the bar graph to make sure that they understand what it shows. For example:

- Is this a vertical or horizontal bar graph?
- What does the graph show?
- How many pupils does each block (or mark on the y-axis) represent?

Unit 79 gives the students more practice at reading bar graphs, but this time the graphs are horizontal and not vertical. Look at the first graph on page 84 with the students to make sure that they understand what it shows. Students can then complete the questions in Units 78 and 79.

Ask the students about what they would collect data on. Ask the students for their ideas. Tell them that it must be easy to do, but that they can use observing, interviewing, or both techniques to collect their data. Examples include:

- How do people on my street get to work or school?
- What pets do people own in my neighbourhood?
- Which types of vehicle pass your house on one day?

Once the students have decided which question they will collect data about, they need to decide how they will collect this data, when they will collect it, whether they need help or not, and finally how they will represent their data (either as a pictograph or a bar graph). Let the students work through these questions on their own, but give them guidance if they ask for it.

Once students have finished planning their data collection, go through each one with them to make sure that it is possible and safe to do.

Once the project is completed, students could give a short presentation about their project, explaining why they chose their questions, how they collected the data and how and why they chose to represent it in the way they did.

Unit 80 Review

Objectives

Students should be able to:
- compare linear measurements
- write numbers as words and use expanded notation
- multiply by 1 and 0.

Suggested approach

Use Unit 80 to test the skills listed above. If you wish to assess work on pictographs, provide a similar pictograph to those in Units 78 and 79, and ask students similar questions about it.

Unit 81 Comparing fractions

Objectives

Students should be able to:
- identify numerator and denominator
- identify fractions of a group or whole
- place unit fractions in serial order
- order fractions with the same numerator.
- use < and > to compare two fractions
- recognise equivalent fractions

Suggested approach

Write the word 'fractions' on the board. Write the following fraction on the board: $1/3$. Ask the class if they know what we call the top part of the fraction (the numerator). Write the word 'numerator' on the board. Then ask if they know what we call the bottom part of the fraction (the denominator). Next to $1/3$, draw a circle, and divide it into three equal segments. Colour in one of the segments. Explain that this is a third of the circle, or one of three equal parts. Point to the fraction again, and explain that the denominator represents the number of equal parts that make up the whole, and the numerator represents how many of those parts we are counting. Get the students to come up to the board and write their own fractions. They should illustrate each fraction with a shaded diagram. Ask them to identify the numerator and denominator in each fraction.

Unit-by-unit support

Draw a circle on the board. Divide it into four equal parts, and ask the students to identify what fraction we would use to describe one of these parts (a quarter). Then divide the circle again, and ask what fraction we would use to describe one of the equal parts now (an eighth). Ask students which fraction is bigger: a quarter or an eighth? (A quarter.) They should realise that the bigger the denominator, the smaller the fraction. Write the following fractions on the board: $1/3$, $1/7$.

Ask one of the students to come up to the board to fill in a < or > sign. Students may have difficulty with this concept, as they are used to ordering whole numbers. Explain that they should think of fractions as parts of a concrete whole, such as a cake or pie. The more pieces we divide the cake into, the smaller each piece. Give some more examples for students to fill in the sign < or >.

Students can then complete the questions in Unit 81. Then let them work through questions 1 and 2 of the additional activities that follow.

Draw a circle on the board, and draw lines to divide it into five equal parts. Shade one of the parts, and ask the students to identify what we would call this fraction. (One-fifth.) Then shade another of the parts, and ask the students what we would call the shaded area. (Two-fifths.) Demonstrate with a few more examples. Then let students complete question 3 of the additional activities that follow.

CD-Rom activity
- Comparing fractions

Additional activities
Ordering and comparing fractions
1 Fill in < or >.
   a $1/2$ ___ $1/5$ b $1/8$ ___ $1/3$ c $1/9$ ___ $1/20$
   d $1/3$ ___ $1/4$ e $1/7$ ___ $1/20$
2 Write each set of fractions in order from smallest to largest.
   a $1/4$, $1/2$, $1/10$ b $1/7$, $1/10$, $1/5$ c $1/2$, $1/25$, $1/9$, $1/10$, $1/5$
3 Write each set of fractions in order from smallest to largest.
   a $6/7$, $5/7$, $3/7$, $1/7$ b $1/8$, $5/8$, $3/8$ c $9/10$, $2/10$, $3/10$, $7/10$

Units 82 to 86   Division

Materials
- bottle caps

Objectives
Students should be able to:
- divide a two-digit number by a one-digit number without remainders
- use division to find out how many members are in equivalent sets
- solve division problems, using the correct symbols
- know and use the relationship between × and ÷ tables.

Suggested approach

Give each student about 20 bottle caps. Write the following number sentence on the board: 6 ÷ 2 = ___. Question students to find out if they know how to work out the answer.

Ask them to take six objects and put them in sets of two. Ask: How many sets are there? (Three.) Let one student draw six objects on the board and divide them into two equal sets of three. Let another student complete the number sentence: 6 ÷ 2 = 3. Encourage the whole class to read the number sentence.

Write this number sentence on the board: 12 ÷ 3 = ___. Repeat the procedure described above. Do other examples.

Write the following number sentence on the board: 15 ÷ 3 = ___. Let a student draw 15 objects on the board. Another student should divide the set of 15 into equal sets of three and complete the number sentence. Then ask: How many sets are there? (Five.) Let students work on other examples in the same way. Then let them complete Unit 82. For questions 1 to 4, they should work out the problems using the pictures to help them. For question 5, they should draw shapes in their exercise books in order to work out the divisions.

Repeat the procedure above, using bottle caps to demonstrate division, but use other number sentences. Then write the following word problem on the board:
- Mother has 15 peanuts to give away. She gives five peanuts to each of her children. To how many children did she give peanuts?

Let a student read the problem aloud. Ask: How would you solve this problem? Allow a student to write the number sentence on the board. Let another student draw objects to help them find the answer and complete the number sentence: 15 ÷ 5 = 3. Work out other problems using the same procedure. Let students read the example at the top of Unit 83. Students should draw little dots to represent the seeds in question 1, in order to work out each division sum. In question 2, they should draw their own shapes.

Unit 84 follows the same principle, although students should draw simple flowers for each vase. They should work in their exercise books, as there is not enough space to draw the flowers on page 89 in the Pupil Book. In Unit 85, they can work in the Pupil Book.

The 'talk about' box on page 90 asks students how they can use multiplication to help them to check their answers. Students should realise that they can multiply the quotient by the divisor, and this should give the dividend. You may want to give students this vocabulary using an example such as 12 ÷ 3 = 4. In this problem, 12 is the dividend, 3 is the divisor and 4 is the quotient. In order to check the problem, we can multiply the quotient (4) by the divisor (3) in order to get the dividend (12).

Unit 86 deals with dividing bigger numbers. The example at the top of the page introduces this concept by using repeated subtraction. Go through this example with the students and do a few more of your own.

Each time, show the students how they can check their answers using multiplication.

Question 3 requires the students to say what the remainder will be in each case. Go through the example first before you let students attempt to answer the questions.

Units 87 to 92 — Numbers and operations

Materials
- bottle caps
- hundred chart

Objectives

Students should be able to:

- ✓ use several strategies to recall basic facts related to multiplication and division
- ✓ solve problems involving addition of whole numbers, with totals up to 999
- ✓ solve problems involving subtraction of numbers with up to three digits
- ✓ identify odd and even numbers
- ✓ estimate and check addition and subtraction problems
- ✓ work with a number line
- ✓ solve problems involving addition and subtraction in the same problem.

Suggested approach

Ask each student to make a set of two bottle caps. Ask: How many sets do you have? (One.) How many bottle caps do you have? (Two.) Write this on the board:

$1 \times 2 = 2$

Ask students to take another set of two bottle caps. Ask: How many sets of two bottle caps do you have now? (Two.) Ask: How many bottle caps do you have altogether? (Four.) Write this on the board:

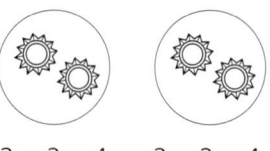

$2 + 2 = 4 \qquad 2 \times 2 = 4$

Let the students read the number sentences as: two plus two equals four; two groups or sets of two equals four. Continue in the same way up to ten sets of two.

Write some incomplete number sentences on the board. For example:

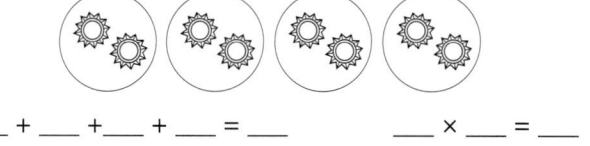

___ + ___ + ___ + ___ = ___   ___ × ___ = ___

Let the students complete them. Then let students complete question 1 in Unit 87. Question 2 deals with simple addition and problem solving. Students should be able to complete this question without any introductory activities.

Select six students to stand in front of the class. Then put them in pairs and let each pair hold hands. Ask: How many children are there altogether? (Six.) Does each child have a partner? (Yes.) Now let five different children come forward and repeat the procedure. This time one of the children will not have a partner.

Draw two columns on the board, one headed 'Numbers that can be put in pairs' and the other headed 'Numbers that cannot be put in pairs'. Ask another group of students to come forward and find out for themselves the number of students in their group, and whether or not they can be put in pairs. Write the number in the correct column. Repeat several times. Keep the columns on the board.

Draw between ten and 15 crosses on the board and ask if any of the students can show whether the crosses can be put in pairs with no remainder. The easiest way to do this is to draw circles around pairs of crosses. Then let one of the students count the number of crosses and write the number in the appropriate column. Repeat several times.

Tell the class that when a number of objects can be grouped in twos with no remainder, that number is called an even number. But when the number cannot be grouped in twos with no remainder, that number is called an odd number. Write the headings 'Even numbers' and 'Odd numbers' at the tops of the columns on the board.

Let the students make sets of bottle caps of any size they like, and then group the bottle caps in twos. Ask several students to tell you the number of bottle caps in their sets, and whether the number is even or odd. Write the numbers they name in the appropriate columns on the board. Clean the board before the students complete Unit 88.

Let the students talk about what they studied in the previous lesson – odd and even numbers. Draw this on the board:

⊖⊖ ⊖⊖ ⊖⊖ ⊖⊖

Let the students say how many marbles there are, and whether the number is odd or even. Let them explain why. Draw one more marble:

⊖⊖ ⊖⊖ ⊖⊖ ⊖⊖ ⊖

Let the students say why the number is odd.

Write on the board: 1, 3, 5, 7, 9, 11, __, __, __, __, __. Let the students say whether the numbers are odd or even, and what the next five odd numbers are. Now do the same with even numbers: 2, 4, 6, 8, 10, __, __, __, __, __. Let the students list the next five even numbers. Then let them complete two other examples: 24, 26, 28, __, __, __; 41, 43, 45, __, __, __.

Write on the board: 20, 21, 22, 23, 24, 25, 26, 27, 28, 29, 30. Let the

Unit-by-unit support 63

CD-Rom activity
- Odd and even numbers

students read the numbers. Ask a student to write all the odd numbers between 20 and 30. Discuss the answer with the class. Then discuss the even numbers between 20 and 30.

Write on the board: 2 + 1 = ___. Ask the students to say whether the answer is odd or even. Let them add, then check. Do some other examples, then let students complete Unit 89.

Unit 90 deals with division problems. Students have dealt with dividing bigger numbers in Unit 86. Go through the example at the top of page 95, reminding the students that they can use repeated to subtraction to help them. Give the students some word problems of your own to solve for practice, or you can ask students to make up their own problems to give to a partner to solve.

Read through the questions in Unit 90 with the students before asking them to complete the page.

In Unit 91, students explore the relationship between addition and subtraction. Tell students to take a set of five bottle caps, then a set of seven bottle caps. Let them put the set of seven with the set of five. Ask a student to write the corresponding number sentence on the board: 5 + 7 = 12. Ask another student to read the number sentence aloud. Repeat with other examples, using some subtraction, for example: 7 + 5 = 12; 12 − 7 = 5; 12 − 5 = 7.

Write a number sentence on the board and ask the students to use their bottle caps to find the answer, for example: 8 + 3 = __; 11 − 8 = __. Repeat with other examples.

- Write a word problem on the board, for example: Johnny has 8 lemons and 4 mangoes. How many fruits has Johnny altogether?

Let the students read out the problem, suggest ways to solve it, and write out the complete number sentence. Repeat with other examples. Then let students work through Unit 91.

The 'talk about' box in Unit 91 asks students to consider the relationships between the numbers in addition and subtraction sums. Students should realise that the numbers in an addition sum are interchangeable, but the numbers in a subtraction problem are not.

In Unit 92, students work on problems with more than one operation in the number sentence. Go through the example at the top of Unit 92, getting the students to work with the number line to solve the problems. Then let them work through questions 1 to 3. You may also want to let students make up their own word problems involving more than one operation.

The 'talk about' box in Unit 92 can be used as a discussion point, or as a starting point for independent research. You could arrange for a librarian (from the school library, or from a local public library) to speak to the students about the filing system. Most libraries use the Dewey Decimal system. The librarian will be able to explain how to find the reference number of a book, and how to find the book on the shelf.

Units 93 and 94 — Capacity

Materials
- water
- enough half-litre and litre containers for each group of four to six students to have one litre container and two half-litre containers

Objectives

Students should be able to:
- ✓ work with litres and half-litres
- ✓ use <, > and = to compare the capacity of groups of containers.

Suggested approach

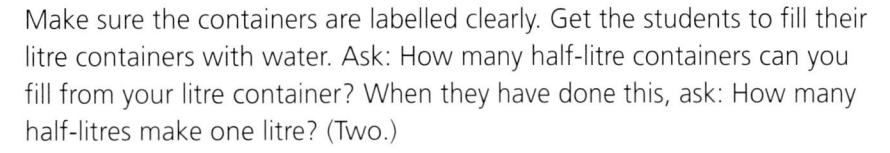

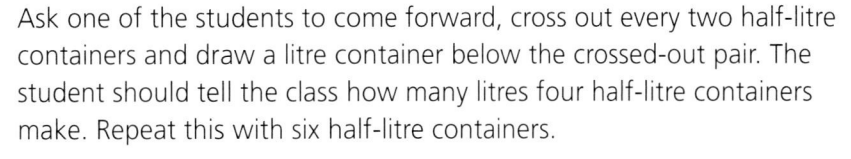

Make sure the containers are labelled clearly. Get the students to fill their litre containers with water. Ask: How many half-litre containers can you fill from your litre container? When they have done this, ask: How many half-litres make one litre? (Two.)

Draw this on the board.

Ask one of the students to come forward, cross out every two half-litre containers and draw a litre container below the crossed-out pair. The student should tell the class how many litres four half-litre containers make. Repeat this with six half-litre containers.

Draw this on the board.

Ask students to tell you how many litres are shown. (Four and a half.) Let them explain how they reached their answer. Repeat with other examples.

Tell the class that we have used litre bottles and half-litre bottles to measure water. Then ask: What other items do we usually measure in litres? Let students suggest items and write the list on the board. Then let them work through Unit 93.

The 'talk about' box on page 98 invites the students to think about how much water they use for certain activities in one day. This will help them to estimate capacity in an everyday context.

Use the bottles to make different combinations of litre and half-litre containers. Let the students suggest the total capacity of each set. Once they are easily working out the capacity of each set, draw this on the board:

Let the students tell you the capacity of each set of containers. Then ask them to say which set has a bigger capacity. Let them select the correct symbol, <, > or = to compare the two sets. Repeat with several other examples. Also ask students to draw bottles to make statements using the symbols <, > and =, for example:

Unit-by-unit support

When students have had some practice making and solving capacity problems, they can complete Unit 94.

Units 95 and 96 — Addition

Objectives

Students should be able to:
- ✓ solve addition problems using regrouping
- ✓ add three two-digit numbers.

Suggested approach

Write a number sentence on the board, for example: 15 + 19 = ___.

Draw a tally chart below it. Ask one of the students to represent the two numbers by making tally marks in the tally chart. The drawings on the board should look like that on the left.

tens	ones
|	|||||
|	|||||||||

15 + 19 = ____

Ask the student: How many tens are there altogether? (Two.) How many ones are there? (14.) Encourage the students to draw a ring around ten ones and to represent it as another ten. Draw attention to the fact that this makes three tens, and four ones. Ask the student to insert the correct number of tallies in the box underneath. Ask: How do we write that? Repeat this procedure with several examples. You should also use word problems for some of the examples. Then let students complete Unit 95.

Repeat the procedure above, but use three two-digit numbers instead of two two-digit numbers. For example, 26 + 13 + 19 = ___. Repeat this with some different examples. Then let students work through Unit 96.

Unit 97 — Operations on fractions

Objectives

Students should be able to:
- ✓ add two proper fractions with like denominators
- ✓ solve problems involving addition of fractions and fractions of a group of objects.

Suggested approach

Students dealt with adding fractions in level 2, but may need a reminder. Draw a rectangle on the board and divide it into eighths. Shade in $1/8$. Ask the students what fraction of the rectangle you have shaded in.

Now shade in three more eighths in a different colour. Ask the students how many eighths you shaded in this time. ($^3/_8$.) Ask the students how many eighths have been shaded in altogether. ($^4/_8$.) Write this on the board:

$$^1/_8 + {^3/_8} = {^4/_8}$$

Explain to the students that they can add and subtract the numerators of fractions if the denominators are the same.

Draw a circle on the board, and draw radii dividing the circle into quarters. Ask questions such as:
- How many parts are there? (Four.)
- If I take one part away, what fraction am I taking? (One-quarter.)
- What fraction is left? (Three-quarters.)

Repeat with shapes divided into sevenths, fifths and so on. Go through the example at the top of Unit 97 and then ask the students to complete the questions on this page.

Units 98 to 100 Review and assessment

Objectives

Students should be able to:
- ✓ work with litres and half-litres
- ✓ use <, > and = to compare the capacity of groups of containers
- ✓ divide whole numbers, using objects and shapes to help with division
- ✓ differentiate between even and odd numbers
- ✓ add three numbers
- ✓ round off to the nearest ten
- ✓ estimate, measure and compare length
- ✓ read and write prices
- ✓ work out the total cost of a group of similarly priced items
- ✓ work with sets
- ✓ use the vocabulary associated with sets
- ✓ solve word problems involving division.

Suggested approach

Use Units 98 to 100 to assess the work done in Units 81 to 97. Students will need extra paper to do their workings – for example, to draw shapes to solve division problems and to write addition and subtraction problems out in full. Note that activity 1 in Unit 99 is a practical activity involving measuring. Students can work in pairs on this activity. They will need tape measures or metre rules to mark out the full distance, as well as chalk, pegs or markers to mark the start and finish points (a labelled tin, golf peg or simple flag would work well). Read through the instructions carefully and make sure that the students understand what to do.

Question 2 in Unit 99 requires students to go to a shop and find out prices of grocery items. They could do this for homework, or you might want to arrange a class outing to a nearby shop.

If a student is having difficulty with a particular question, return to the unit covering that material and give the student more examples to work through.

Units 101 and 102 — 3D shapes

Materials
- examples of solids with different numbers of faces and vertices

Objectives
Children should be able to:
- ✓ sort examples of the cube, cuboid, cylinder, cone and sphere
- ✓ identify the similarities between the cube and cuboid
- ✓ identify the vertices of 3D shapes
- ✓ describe 3D faces in terms of the number of vertices and the type of faces.

Suggested approach

Students should now be quite familiar with cubes, cuboids, cylinders, cones and spheres. In these two units they have to be able to explain the difference between the shapes.

Ask the students to name some examples of each type of shape. Some examples include:
- cube: boxes, playing blocks, dice
- sphere: ball of cheese, football, tennis ball, melon, apple
- cuboid: matchbox, pencil tin, cereal box
- cylinder: tin, roll of wrapping paper, toilet paper
- cone: party hat, ice-cream cone

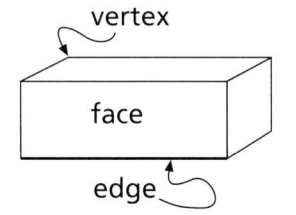

Draw a cuboid on the board and label it as shown.

Explain that when we talk about solid shapes, the surfaces of the shape are called faces. Point out that cubes and cuboids have six flat faces. Ask how cubes and cuboids are different. Students should be able to tell you that all the faces of a cube are square. The faces of a cuboid are rectangular, although some cuboids may have two square faces. Ask the students to describe the faces of a cylinder. (It has two flat faces and one curved face.) Explain that the line where two faces meet is called an edge. Where three or more edges meet, a corner or point is formed. Another name for a point is a vertex.

Ask students to complete the questions in Units 101 and 102.

The 'talk about' box on page 107 asks students how many ways they could sort the shapes in question 1 into two groups. Listen to the students' ideas and make sure that they can explain their reasoning. Expect answers that involve number of sides, number of curved surfaces, and so on.

Units 103 to 107 Multiplication

Materials
- hundred chart
- counters
- 30 bottle caps per student

Objectives

Students should be able to:
- ✓ discover, memorise and recall multiplication facts
- ✓ find unknown factors or products using number lines, arrays and facts
- ✓ explain the commutative property of factors in a multiplication sentence
- ✓ multiply a two-digit number by 10 and 100
- ✓ understand multiplication as repeated addition
- ✓ compare products using < or >
- ✓ use rounded numbers to estimate products.

Suggested approach

Ask students to make two sets or groups of three bottle caps. Record the answer on the board. Then ask the students to make three sets of two bottle caps. Again, record the answer on the board:

$$2 \times 3 = 6 \quad 3 \times 2 = 6.$$

Draw the students' attention to the two number sentences and ask them what they notice (the answers are the same):

$$2 \times 3 = 3 \times 2.$$

Write the following number sentences on the board and let the students find the answers: $4 \times 3 =$ ___; $3 \times 4 =$ ___. Question students about the answers, and help them see the relationship between the two number sentences, that $3 \times 4 = 4 \times 3 = 12$. Do another example. Repeat the same procedure, but get the students to draw sets of objects on the board instead of using bottle caps. Then let students work through Unit 103.

Draw a number line on the board. Number it 0 to 20. Write the following word problem on the board:
- Five girls go to the library. Each girl takes out two books. How many books do the girls take out altogether?

Ask the class how we would work out the answer. Let one student write the number sentence on the board: $5 \times 2 =$ ___. Ask another student to show five sets of two on the number line:

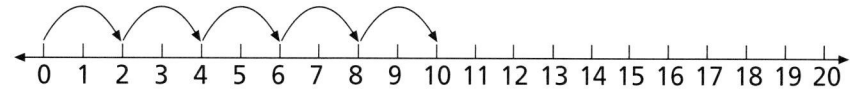

Unit-by-unit support

Encourage another student to start at zero and make five sets of two spaces. Let another student complete the number sentence: 5 × 2 = 10. Do other examples in the same way. Concentrate on multiplication by 2, 5 and 10.

Do some more examples in the same way as above, but get students to draw the groups in different ways on the number line. For example, for 3 × 4, they can move forward three spaces, four times. Then they can move forwards four spaces, three times. Do this with some different examples. Then let students complete Unit 104.

The 'talk about' box draws students' attention to the relationship between the numbers in a multiplication problem. They should realise by now that the order in which the factors are arranged (3 × 4 or 4 × 3) does not change the product.

Divide the class into groups of three. Give each group about 100 bottle caps. Ask the groups to make a set of ten bottle caps. Then ask: How many sets of ten do you have? (One.) How many bottle caps do you have altogether? (Ten.) Draw the set shown below on the board.

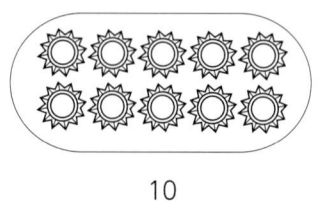

10
1 × 10 = 10

Let the students make another set of ten bottle caps. Ask: How many sets do you have? (Two.) How many bottle caps do you have altogether? (20.) Continue up to ten sets of ten. Then let students complete Unit 105.

Unit 106 extends multiplying by 10. Write the following on the board:

1 × 10 = 10
2 × 10 = 20
3 × 10 = 30

Continue this until 15 × 10 = 150. Ask the students if they notice any pattern in the answers. The students will probably say that you can just add a zero to the number that you are multiplying by 10. Help them to see that the number you are multiplying by 10 moves up one place unit. For example in 2 × 10, the two ones becomes two tens and there are no ones. Another way to think of this is to multiply by 1 and add a zero for the ten.

Give the students some bigger numbers to multiply by ten to see if they can apply this pattern.

Turn to Unit 106 and ask the students to complete the questions on this page.

Unit 107 builds on the place value theory touched on in Unit 106 by using it to multiply by 100. Start recreating the place value table at the top of page 112. Start by writing 1 × 100 on the left-hand side and fill in the hundreds, tens and ones column. Then write 2 × 100, but this time ask a student to fill in the digits in the place value table. Continue until you have completed the table for 12 × 100.

Ask the students what they notice about the table. They should be able to see that there are only zeros in the tens and ones columns and that the number that they are multiplying by 100 has moved up two place values. Make sure that the students can explain what is happening in their own words, as this will help their understanding. Again, another way to think of this is to multiply by 1 and add a zero for each power of ten. In this case it would be two zeros.

Students can then complete the questions in Unit 107.

Additional activities

Comparing products of multiplication problems

Students in Jamaica need to compare the products of multiplication problems using < and >. Teachers can give the class pairs of simple multiplication problems and ask them to compare the answers using < and >. Students in this area also need to use rounded off numbers to estimate products. Teachers should give students examples of multiplication problems involving two- or three-digit numbers. Here are some examples.

1 Estimate the answers to each multiplication problem by rounding off the first number to the nearest 5. Then work out the accurate answer.
   a 17 × 9   **b** 23 × 2   **c** 49 × 4   **d** 88 × 3
2 Estimate the answers to each multiplication problem by rounding off the first number to the nearest 10. Then work out the accurate answer.
   a 192 × 3   **b** 433 × 2   **c** 203 × 4   **d** 312 × 2

Multiplication facts and number patterns

Students in Jamaica are required to organise multiplication facts into a chart. They are also required to generate number patterns using the four operations and to represent these numbers on a hundred chart. The following activities cover these requirements.

1 Work in pairs. Draw three columns on a large sheet of paper, with the headings 'Answers divisible by 3', 'Answers divisible by 5' and 'Answers divisible by 4'. Work out the answer to each multiplication sum, then write the completed number sentence in the correct columns. Some answers can go in more than one column.

   4 × 3   8 × 5   9 × 6   7 × 8   2 × 2   15 × 2   6 × 10
   9 × 9   7 × 7   5 × 3   7 × 6   4 × 9   8 × 3   5 × 5

2 **a** For this activity, you will need a hundred chart and some counters. Choose a number less than 5. Multiply the number by 2. Put a counter on your answer. Then multiply the answer by 2. Put a counter on your answer. Keep doing this until your answer goes over 100. Try to describe the pattern your counters make on the hundred chart.
   b Now choose an operation (multiplication, division, addition or subtraction) and use that operation to create your own number pattern on the 100 chart.

Units 108 to 111 — Shapes and perimeter

Materials
- chart with different shapes
- cut-outs of shapes
- small mirror
- string
- rulers
- tape measures
- metre rules

Objectives

Students should be able to:
- identify plane shapes including squares, circles, triangles, rectangles (and to describe squares, rectangles and triangles in terms of the number and length of their sides), pentagons and hexagons
- identify and draw lines of symmetry in shapes and objects
- explain what a line of symmetry is
- explain the concept of perimeter
- estimate, measure and calculate perimeter.

Suggested approach

Show the chart with the different shapes. Ask students to name the shapes they know. They should recognise circles, squares, triangles and rectangles. Ask them to describe squares, rectangles and triangles in terms of the number and length of their sides (for example, a square is a shape with four sides of equal length; a rectangle also has four sides but two are longer). If necessary introduce the names of less common shapes, such as pentagon, hexagon, heptagon, and so on. Draw attention to the root '-gon' which comes from the Greek word for angles. So, for example, heptagon comes from the Greek 'hepta', meaning seven, and 'gon', meaning angled, as the shape has seven interior angles.

Ask the class if they know the word 'symmetry'. Write the word on the board. If possible, get one of the students to explain the meaning of symmetry, using cut-outs to demonstrate. If no-one can explain, show the class a cut-out of a circle. Fold the circle in half along a diameter. Ask the class what they notice about the way it folds. They should notice that the sides mirror each other. Open out the circle again, and lay the flat edge of the mirror along the diameter so that one side is reflected in the mirror. Explain to the students that when you draw a line of symmetry through a shape, both sides form mirror-images of each other. We say that these shapes are symmetrical. A shape has a line of symmetry if it can be folded in half and the two halves are exactly the same.

Give the students some cut-outs of shapes and ask them to put those that have a line of symmetry into one pile and the shapes that do not into another pile. Remind them that they can fold the shapes to find out whether they are symmetrical.

Let students complete Units 108 and 109.

The 'talk about' box in Unit 108 asks students whether their bodies are symmetrical. Bodies are not really symmetrical, but it is possible to draw an outline to make the body look symmetrical. It is also possible to make symmetrical and asymmetrical poses using the body – for example, standing with legs apart, arms to the sides and head facing forward is a symmetrical pose, whereas standing on one leg is an asymmetrical pose.

CD-Rom activity
- Lines of symmetry

The 'talk about' box in Unit 109 invites students to investigate the number of lines of symmetry in different shapes. They should find that a square has four lines of symmetry (one horizontal, one vertical and two diagonals). Students may have fun with a circle as it has infinite lines of symmetry.

Write the word 'perimeter' on the board. Ask students to volunteer definitions. Perimeter comes from the Greek 'peri-', meaning 'around' and 'metros' meaning 'measure'. Demonstrate how to measure the perimeter of shapes. Draw a regular shape, such as a rectangle, on the board. Then use a metre rule to measure each side, and add the lengths of the sides. Explain that to find the perimeter of a straight-sided shape, we add up the lengths of the sides. Draw a circle on the board. Ask students how we could measure the length of the circumference. Let them give some suggestions. Elicit the suggestion of using string to measure around the circumference. Demonstrate how to do this, then measure the string against a metre rule. Then let students work through the practical activities in Unit 110.

Explain to students that when we do not know a measurement, we can guess it. Another word for a guess is an estimate. Let students work in groups to estimate and measure the items in the table in Unit 111.

Units 112 to 122 Number concept and operations

Materials
- real or cardboard coins
- items from the classroom shop
- cards with simple problems on one side and answers on the back
- dice
- counters

Objectives

Students should be able to:
- work out the total value of a set of coins or notes
- count change from notes or coins in common use
- solve money problems
- represent different amounts of money
- use vocabulary related to spending
- define and use vocabulary related to numbers
- order numbers
- relate division to multiplication
- write pairs of multiplication and division facts
- use multiplication to check the answer to a division sum
- use operations to solve word sums
- use repeated subtraction to divide a two-digit number by a one-digit number with and without remainders
- use several strategies to recall basic multiplication and division facts
- write story sums and use multiplication or division to solve them.

Suggested approach

Divide the class into groups of four. Ask the groups to use any combination of coins to make up 40c. Repeat the activity for the following amounts: 45c, 60c, 65c, 75c, 90c.

Draw the following coins on the board: 25c, 25c, 25c, 10c, 10c, 5c. Let the students work out the total. ($1.00.) Display an item that costs 60c. Tell the students that Mike bought this item. Call a student to the board to cross out coins that make up 60c. Ask: What do the remaining coins represent? (The change, 40c.) Repeat this procedure with other examples.

Write the following word problem on the board:
- Sammy had 90c. He bought a cake for 75c. What was his change?

Discuss with the class that they must make a combination of coins for 90c so that they can deduct 75c. Let the students use their coins to work it out. Then show on the board: 25c, 25c, 25c, 10c, 5c. Let a student cross out coins that make 75c, and let the class check the change: 10c + 5c = 15c.

Help the class to read through the example at the top of Unit 112. Question 1 requires students to apply their skills of addition with regrouping. Question 2 follows the same pattern as the examples you demonstrated above.

In Unit 113, students work out price totals. In fact, this exercise is a set of word problems requiring addition with and without regrouping. If necessary, do the first question as an example. Get a student to write the number sentence and to solve the addition.

Ask students to look at the words on page 119 in the Pupil Book. Ask individual students to volunteer a definition for each word. Then let the class complete Unit 114 as a fun individual activity. Write the following words on the board: pair, gross, score, triple. Get students to look up definitions for these words in a dictionary, and give examples of when we would use these words.

---

hundreds	tens	ones
)))	))))	)))))
))))	))	)))))

Draw this on the board. Call a student to the board to write the first number shown in the tally chart (346). Call another student to the board to write the next number shown (425). Let the students say which number is larger (425). Ask why it is larger. Students should realise that four hundreds is larger than three hundreds.

Show other examples where the digit in the hundreds place of one number is larger than the digit in the hundreds place of the other numbers, for example 582 and 429; 601 and 243; 199 and 738.

Follow the same procedure as above, helping students to compare the following pairs of numbers: 416 and 420; 388 and 372; 607 and 648; 234 and 237; 783 and 788; 719 and 714; 96 and 142; 82 and 317; 16 and 100. Then let students complete Unit 115.

Draw a number line on the board and number it from 0 to 20. Write the following number sentence on the board: 6 × 2 = ___. Let a student find the answer on the number line. Write the following number sentence on the board: 12 ÷ 2 = ___. Let another student find the answer using the number line as shown below.

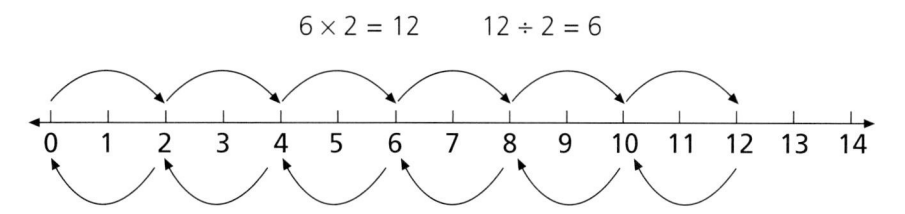

$$6 \times 2 = 12 \qquad 12 \div 2 = 6$$

```
 0  1  2  3  4  5  6  7  8  9  10  11  12  13  14
```

Do other examples in the same way. Then let students complete Units 116 and 117.

In Unit 118, students revise some of the vocabulary related to numbers. Let them work through this unit in pairs. When everyone has finished, go through the unit with the class and explain any words that students do not know.

The 'talk about' box asks students to think of proverbs or sayings about numbers. Expect answers such as: 'A stitch in time saves nine', 'A bird in the hand is worth two in the bush', 'Cats have nine lives', and so on. Encourage students to explain their sayings clearly and to give examples of when you could use that saying or proverb.

Units 119 and 120 offer word problems that give students some practice in basic operations – addition, subtraction, multiplication and division. Students should be able to solve these problems easily at this stage. For Unit 121, students can play in groups of two to four. Each group will need a pile of problem cards – cards that have a simple addition, multiplication, division or subtraction sum on one side, and the answer on the other side. Read through the instructions carefully with the class to make sure everyone understands how to play. Then let students play.

Unit 122 is a continuation of the number line work started in Unit 116. You can use this as a review activity to make sure that students are comfortable with addition and subtraction, and to make sure that they understand the relationship between multiplication and division.

Unit-by-unit support

Units 123 to 125 — Review and assessment

> **Objectives**
>
> Students should be able to:
> - ✓ estimate, calculate and compare perimeters of flat objects
> - ✓ find the total of a group of similarly priced items
> - ✓ work out change in cents
> - ✓ identify pairs, half-dozens and dozens
> - ✓ draw shapes with a given perimeter
> - ✓ use vocabulary associated with numbers
> - ✓ compare and order three-digit numbers
> - ✓ multiply by ten
> - ✓ create and solve problems using addition, multiplication, subtraction and division.

Suggested approach

Use Units 123 to 125 for review and assessment. In Unit 123, question 1 deals with measuring perimeter. Students should remember to add the sides to find the perimeter of each shape. They should lay the string as closely along the perimeter of each shape as possible, taking particular care with the circle. Question 2 deals with working out the total cost of similarly priced items and working out change. By now, students should be able to do this without using coins. Question 3 tests students' knowledge of number-related vocabulary, such as 'pair', 'half-dozen' and 'dozen'. Have a short discussion about the kinds of things we buy in dozens (fruit, bread rolls, and so on) and get students to identify what makes up a half-dozen and quarter-dozen.

In Unit 124, students are expected to draw two shapes that each have a perimeter of 16 cm. Get one of the students to measure the sides of one of the blocks, which measure 1 cm × 1 cm. The easiest shapes would be squares and rectangles, so encourage students to think about how many sides they will draw, and how they can work out which shapes they can draw. Question 2 deals again with number-related vocabulary.

In Unit 125, question 1 asks students to compare three-digit numbers. By now, students should have a firm grasp of place value and should understand that they should first compare hundreds, then tens, then units when ordering three-digit numbers. You may allow them to use extra paper to make tally charts. Question 2 involves multiplying one-digit numbers by ten. Students should understand that they can simply multiply by one and put an extra zero for each power of ten. In question 3, students have an opportunity to create their own problems using each of the basic operations.

Additional activities

Division with remainders

Students in St Lucia and Trinidad need to divide one- and two-digit numbers by one-digit numbers with remainders. The questions below cover this requirement. Go through a few examples with the class before letting them work through these problems.

1 Find the quotient and remainder.
   a 198 ÷ 5
   b 149 ÷ 3
   c 349 ÷ 5
   d 151 ÷ 2
   e 245 ÷ 8
   f 790 ÷ 9

Division of numbers with up to four digits

Students in Jamaica need to divide numbers with up to four digits by 2, 3, 4, 5 and 6. Jamaican teachers can use the problems below to drill long division with three- and four-digit numbers. Go through a few examples with the class before letting them work through these problems.

1 Find the quotient.
   a 168 ÷ 3
   b 276 ÷ 4
   c 225 ÷ 5
   d 150 ÷ 2
   e 198 ÷ 2
   f 365 ÷ 5

2 Find the quotient.
   a 1 475 ÷ 5
   b 2 076 ÷ 3
   c 1 536 ÷ 2
   d 1 458 ÷ 3
   e 1 872 ÷ 4
   f 2 750 ÷ 5

Units 126 to 130 Division and operations

Materials
- bottle caps
- small objects (such as buttons or stones)
- several egg-boxes (each designed to hold six eggs)
- lollipop sticks

Objectives

Students should be able to:
- ✓ recall basic division facts
- ✓ use several strategies to recall basic multiplication and division facts
- ✓ solve division as repeated subtraction and inverse of multiplication
- ✓ use operations to solve problems.

Suggested approach

Give each student about 20 bottle caps. Write the following number sentence on the board: 6 ÷ 2 = __. Ask the class how they would work out the answer. Ask the students to take six objects and put them in sets of two. Ask the students how many sets there are. (Three.) Let one student draw six squares or crosses on the board and draw rings around sets of two. Let another student complete the number sentence: 6 ÷ 2 = 3. Encourage the whole class to read the number sentence.

Write the following number sentence on the board: 12 ÷ 3 = __. Repeat the procedure described above and repeat again using other examples.

Write the following number sentence on the board: 15 ÷ 3 = __. Let a student draw 15 crosses on the board. Let another student divide the crosses into sets of three and complete the number sentence. Then ask:

Unit-by-unit support

How many sets are there altogether? (Five.) Let students work out other examples in the same way.

Then let students work through Unit 126.

Draw a number line on the board and number it from 0 to 20. Write the following number sentence on the board: 20 ÷ 5 = __.

Let a student draw an arrow from the point marked 0 to the point marked 20 on the number line. Ask another student to start at 20 and count five spaces backward. Let them then draw an arrow from the 20 to the number at the end of the fifth space back. Let them continue in this way until the point marked 0 is reached.

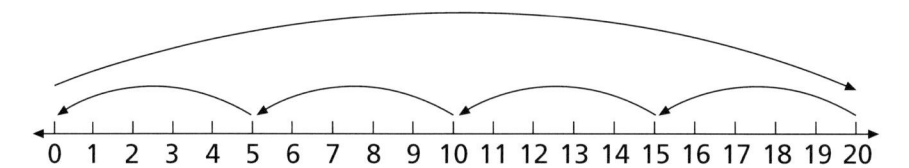

```
 ┌──────────────────────────────────────────┐
 │   ┌──────────────────────────────┐       │
 │   │   ┌──────────────────┐       │       │
 │   │   │   ┌──────┐       │       │       │
 ↓   ↓   ↓   ↓      ↓       ↓       ↓       ↓
 0 1 2 3 4 5 6 7 8 9 10 11 12 13 14 15 16 17 18 19 20
```

The students should now count the number of sets of five and complete the number sentence: 20 ÷ 5 = 4. Then let students complete Unit 127.

Put several egg-boxes on your desk. Point out that each cup in the egg-box holds one egg. Ask: How many eggs does one box hold? (Six.) Say that now we will work out how many boxes we need to hold 18 eggs. Write on the board as shown on the left.

Eggs   **Boxes of 6**
18

Ask one student to count out 18 bottle caps. Ask the class to pretend that each bottle top represents one egg, so if a box contains six bottle caps it is 'full'. Let the student take six of the 18 bottle caps and place one in each egg-box cup. Ask: How many eggs did you take out of the pile to put in the box? (Six.) How many are left in the pile? (12.) Complete the next stage of the algorithm on the board, so that it looks like that on the left.

Eggs   **Boxes of 6**
18
− 6
―――
12

Eggs   **Boxes of 6**
18
− 6   1
―――
12
− 6   1
―――
6
− 6   1
―――
0   3

Ask: How many boxes did you 'fill' with 'eggs'? (One.) Write this into the algorithm on the board, by filling in 1 under the 'Boxes of 6' column. Keep repeating this procedure until the algorithm looks like that on the left.

Count out 21 lollipop sticks and put them in a heap on your desk. Say that you are going to give them in threes to the students in the class. Say that now we will find out how many students get sticks. Write the headings 'Sticks' and 'Students' at the top of the board. Ask one of the students to come forward. Ask: How many sticks are on the table? (21.) Let them write the number 21 on the board just below the heading 'Sticks'. As you hand out sets of three sticks, get the students at the front to keep subtracting three from the column of sticks, until seven students each have a set of three sticks and the algorithm on the board is complete.

Count out 24 bottle caps and put them on your desk. Again, get the students to pretend that bottle caps are eggs. Say that we are going to find out how many boxes we need to contain 24 eggs. Write the headings 'Eggs' and 'Boxes' on the board, and let the students write

CD-Rom activity
- Division

these headings at the top of a page in their exercise books. Count the bottle caps into the boxes, letting the students work in their exercise books, writing out each stage in the algorithm as you 'fill' each box. Then let students work through Units 128 and 129. Then use Unit 130 as a relaxing class activity to revise problem solving using the four operations – multiplication, addition, subtraction and division.

Unit 131 Time

Materials
- calendar

Objectives

Students should be able to:
- ✓ read dates off a calendar
- ✓ state the relationship between units of time, including hours and minutes, years and months, weeks and days
- ✓ use a calendar to determine the duration of an event.

Suggested approach

Show the students the calendar. Ask the following types of questions about how we measure time:
- What month are we in now?
- How many days does this month have?
- How many days are there in one week?
- How many days are there in one year?
- How many months are there in one year?
- How many hours are there in one day?

Write these different units of time on the board (hour, month, year, week, day) and ask the students to put them in order from the shortest unit of time to the longest unit of time.

Unit 131 deals with durations of time. Read through the questions on page 136 to make sure that the students all know what they have to do. They can then complete the unit.

Unit 132 Review

Objectives

Students should be able to:
- ✓ read and write time notation
- ✓ understand am and pm
- ✓ understand the relationship between units of time such as years, days, weeks.

Suggested approach

Use this unit to assess whether students can read and write time notation. If students have difficulty reading or writing the time, give them extra practice using your real or teacher-made clocks.

Unit-by-unit support

Units 133 to 135 Division and fractions

Materials
- egg-boxes
- lollipop sticks
- bottle caps
- cut-outs of shapes such as circles and rectangles

Objectives

Students should be able to:
- ✓ divide a two-digit number by a one-digit number with or without remainders
- ✓ use the language and symbols associated with dividing, grouping and sharing
- ✓ add fractions with like denominators
- ✓ name parts of an object using fractions.

Suggested approach

Refer to the suggested approach for Units 126 to 130 (pages 77–79 of this Teacher's Guide) and use a similar approach here. Give students an example of a simple division problem, and get them to use groups of bottle caps to help them work out the answer using repeated subtraction. Then let them complete Unit 133. They can also use bottle caps to help them work through Unit 134.

The 'talk about' box on page 138 asks the students to use their calculators to check the answers on this page. Students should notice that the answers that they get are not whole numbers. Explain to them that this is because there are remainders in these division problems. The numbers do not divide exactly into each other.

For Unit 135, refer to the suggested approach for Units 21, 22, 46, 47 and 81. Use the cut-outs to demonstrate the principle of equivalent fractions. For example, demonstrate that $1/2 = 2/4 = 4/8$ and so on. Shade $1/4$ of a circle and ask the class: What fraction of the circle is shaded? ($1/4$.) What fraction is unshaded? ($3/4$.) Then let them work through Unit 135.

Additional activities

Comparing similar fractions of different-sized objects

Students in Jamaica need to tell the difference between similar fractions of different-sized objects. Introduce this concept practically by showing two sheets of paper, one larger than the other. Ask: Which piece is bigger? Then fold each sheet of paper in half and ask the students to identify the fractions they have created (halves.) Now ask: Is half of this piece bigger or smaller than half of this piece? Give a few more examples. Then let students work through these questions, either orally or in their exercise books.

1. Which is bigger:
  a $1/2$ of an apple or $1/2$ of a watermelon?
  b $1/3$ of an orange or $1/3$ of a grape?
  c $1/8$ of a small pizza or $1/8$ of a large pizza?
  d $1/4$ of a loaf of bread or $1/4$ of a bread roll?

Mixed numbers, improper fractions and simplification

Students in Jamaica and St Lucia also need to work with mixed numbers, improper fractions and simplification. Write the following fraction on the board: $1^3/_4$. Explain that we sometimes write whole numbers and fractions together as mixed numbers. For example, you might have two loaves of bread, and give away a quarter of one loaf. You would then have $1^3/_4$ loaves. Now ask: How many quarters are there in the whole loaf? (Four.) Instead of writing $1^3/_4$, we could therefore write $^7/_4$. Demonstrate this on the board, and work through a few more examples. Show students how to simplify their answers.

Equivalent fractions

Teachers in St Lucia should allow students to name sets of equivalent fractions using charts and number lines. Also work through some examples of converting improper fractions to mixed numbers. Then let students work through the following problems.

1 Write the following fractions as mixed numbers. Simplify your answer if necessary.
   a $^{20}/_8$ **b** $^{18}/_{10}$ **c** $^{26}/_6$ **d** $^{14}/_3$
   e $^{15}/_4$ **f** $^{28}/_6$ **g** $^{16}/_5$ **h** $^{18}/_7$

2 Write the following mixed numbers as improper fractions.
   a $17^4/_5$ **b** $12^1/_3$ **c** $4^7/_9$ **d** $9^3/_8$
   e $7^3/_5$ **f** $9^7/_8$ **g** $6^2/_7$ **h** $4^1/_3$

3 Write each fraction in its simplest form.
   a $^5/_{15}$ **b** $^4/_{20}$ **c** $^4/_{16}$ **d** $^{12}/_{24}$
   e $^{12}/_{36}$ **f** $^9/_{12}$ **g** $^6/_{60}$ **h** $^{20}/_{100}$

Unit 136 Measurement

Materials
- tape measure
- metre rule
- scale
- measuring jug

Objectives

Students should be able to:
- ✓ select appropriate units of measurement.

Suggested approach

Set out the different measuring instruments on a table. Ask a student to name each of the measuring instruments and to name the two standard units that we use for each instrument. Ask another student to write the name of each unit on the board. For example, for the measuring jug students should name litres and millilitres. Then let students work through Unit 136.

CD-Rom activity
- Measurement

Units 137 and 138 — Shape and space

> **Objectives**
>
> Students should be able to:
> - ✓ identify straight line segments
> - ✓ draw and label line segments
> - ✓ identify curves
> - ✓ explain the concepts of 'open curve' and 'closed curve'
> - ✓ identify and draw open and closed curves.

Suggested approach

Draw a straight line on the board. Tell the students that this is a straight line segment. We know this because it has a beginning point and an end point. Label one end of the line 'S' and the other end 'T'. Tell the students that this line segment is called ST.

Ask a student to come to the board and draw a line segment RS. Repeat the exercise, asking different students to come to the board and draw different line segments.

Now draw a square on the board and label the corners A, B, C, and D. Now number the sides so that AB is 1, BC is 2, CD is 3 and DA is 4. Now ask students questions about these line segments, such as:
- What is the name of line segment 1?
- What number is line segment CD?

Students can then complete the questions in Unit 137.

Draw a straight line and a curved line on the board. Ask the students what we call these two lines. (A straight line and a curved line.) Now draw a closed curved line and an open curved line on the board. Ask the students what the difference between these two curved lines is. They should be able to tell you that an open curved line has a beginning point and an end point, and that in a closed curve, the beginning and end points are joined together.

Ask students to come to the board and draw open and closed curves. They should then be ready to do the questions on page 143.

The 'talk about' box in Unit 138 asks the students to describe closed and open curves in their own words, which they should be able to do, since you have already discussed this question as a class.

Units 139 to 143 Numbers and operations

Materials
- building blocks

Objectives

Students should be able to:
- ✓ use computation strategies for mixed operations
- ✓ select an appropriate strategy (calculator, pencil and paper or mental strategy) to investigate number patterns and relationships
- ✓ identify the pattern in a sequence of numbers
- ✓ estimate and check answers
- ✓ create and solve problems involving money.

Suggested approach

Units 139 to 143 give students an opportunity to practise working with addition, subtraction, multiplication and division in different ways. At this stage, make sure that students are familiar with regrouping in addition and subtraction problems. If any students have difficulty with regrouping, go through some examples using tally charts to remind them how to regroup.

Unit 141 deals with number patterns. Before asking the students to complete the questions on this page, revise counting in 2s, 3s, 4s, 5s, 10s, 20s, 25s, 50s and 100s from any number. You should also revise counting in these steps backwards. In the early stages, students could use building blocks to represent 1s, 10s and 100s.

The 'talk about' box on page 146 invites students to examine the number pattern, and to describe what they notice about it. (Each number increases by nine.) Students may also notice that the right-hand side number decreases by one each time and the left-hand side number increases by one each time.

Units 142 and 143 give students an opportunity to solve real-life problems involving money. They need to understand that these problems work on the same principle as straightforward operations. Once the students have completed Unit 143, ask then to make up some of their own problems that involve money for their partner to solve.

Units 144 and 145 More addition/subtraction with regrouping

Objectives

Students should be able to:
- ✓ add and subtract numbers with up to three digits, with regrouping in two columns/places.

Suggested approach

Units 144 and 145 give the students more practice at regrouping, this time regrouping in two columns/places. Students covered regrouping in two columns when subtracting in Unit 38. Follow this suggested approach to these units.

Go through the examples at the top of Units 144 and 145, reminding the students that ten ones is equal to one ten, and ten tens is equal to one hundred. Students can then complete the questions on these pages.

Units 146 to 150 Review and assessment

Objectives

Students should be able to:
- ✓ add and subtract, with and without regrouping
- ✓ work with simple fractions
- ✓ work with calendars
- ✓ write numbers up to 999 in words and figures
- ✓ write money amounts using the correct notation
- ✓ identify correct units of measurement for different objects
- ✓ identify the number of faces and edges in three-dimensional objects
- ✓ identify straight lines and curved lines
- ✓ solve real-life problems using basic operations
- ✓ solve practical problems involving division and multiplication.

Suggested approach

Units 146 to 150 give you an opportunity to review and assess some of the work covered in Units 135, 136, 137, 138, 144 and 145. You can use these units as class tests, or simply for drilling, depending on which areas you think require further practice.

Level 3 curriculum coverage grid

Pupil Book 3

c = core   n = new objectives for this edition   e = extension

This grid will be updated in the event of future curriculum changes. For more information on the latest grid, please visit www.pearsoncaribbean.com.

Units	Objectives	OECS*	Trinidad & Tobago	Bahamas	Barbados	Jamaica
1 and 2	identify and complete number patterns and sequences	c	c	c	c	c
	identify place value in three- and four-digit numbers	c	c	c	c	c
	tell the total value of any digit in three- and four-digit numbers	c	c	c	c	c
	work with hundreds, tens and ones	c	c	c	c	c
	distinguish between place value and total value	c	c	c	c	c
3 and 4	write numbers up to 999 on place value charts	c	c	n	c	n
	write numerals for numbers up to 999	c	c	n	c	n
5	identify numbers before or after a given number	c	c	c	c	c
	order numbers from smallest to largest and vice versa	c	c	c	c	c
	identify and complete number patterns and sequences	c	c	c	c	c
6 to 9	add a two-digit number to a single-digit number without regrouping	c	c	n	c	n
	subtract a single-digit number from a two-digit number without regrouping	c	c	n	c	n
10 and 11	identify the place value and total value of any digit in two- and three-digit numbers	c	c	c	c	c
	use a calculator to carry out calculations when necessary	c	c	n	n	n
	read numbers up to 999	c	c	n	c	n
	write numbers up to 999 in words and symbols	c	c	n	c	n
12 and 13	estimate, measure and record lengths using standard and non-standard units of measurement	c	c	c	c	c
	explain why there is a need for a smaller unit of measure – the centimetre	c	e	n	n	n
	compare linear measurements of two or three objects	c	c	n	n	n
14 to 18	explain what a tally chart is	c	c	n	n	n
	explain how to use tallies to construct a table	c	c	n	n	n
	use tally charts to organise collected data	c	c	n	n	n
	identify and describe situations in everyday life that involve data collection and data representation, and why people collect data	c	c	n	n	n
	draw and interpret simple pictographs	c	c	c	c	c
	read information from a pictograph	c	c	c	c	c
	collect and represent data	c	c	c	c	c
	describe the characteristics of bar graphs in which one block represents one unit of data	c	c	n	n	n
	compare sets using <, > and = signs	c	c	c	c	c
19	work with calendars	c	e	c	c	c
	solve problems involving addition and subtraction of whole numbers	c	c	n	c	n
20	identify the ordinal position of an object in an arranged set	c	e	n	n	n
	identify the object that is in a given ordinal position in an arranged set	c	e	n	n	n
21 and 22	identify the fraction of a whole or set	c	c	c	c	c
	represent fractions using numbers or pictures	c	c	c	c	c
23 to 25	represent time in different ways	c	c	e	c	c
	read time off an analogue clock to the hour, half-hour and quarter-hour	c	c	c	c	c
26 and 27	read and write time notation	c	c	c	c	c
	use vocabulary associated with time	c	c	c	c	c
	work with counting, basic operations (+ and -) and units of measurements	c	c	n	n	n
	read and interpret information presented on a pictograph	c	c	c	c	c
	identify fractions of a whole or a set	c	c	c	c	c
28 to 31	add two-digit numbers with and without regrouping	c	c	c	c	c
	subtract a one-digit number from a two-digit number with regrouping	c	c	c	c	c
	subtract a two-digit number from another two-digit number without regrouping	c	c	c	c	c
	add two-digit numbers to one- or two-digit numbers with regrouping.	c	c	c	c	c
32 and 33	work with hundreds, tens and units	c	c	c	c	c
	order and compare numbers up to 999	c	c	c	c	c
	skip count in 5s, 10s, 20s, 25s, 100s	c	c	c	c	c
	add 100s	c	c	c	c	c
34 and 35	identify the coins in circulation	c	c	n	c	n
	solve problems involving money	c	c	c	c	c
	make amounts using different combinations of coins	c	c	c	c	c
36	add two-digit numbers with and without regrouping	c	c	c	c	c
	skip count	c	c	c	c	c
	work with money	c	c	c	c	c
37 and 38	subtract a single- or two-digit number from a three-digit number with or without regrouping	c	c	c	c	c

*OECS includes Anguilla, Antigua & Barbuda, British Virgin Islands, Dominica, Grenada, Montserrat, St Kitts & Nevis, St Lucia, St Vincent & the Grenadines

Units	Objectives	OECS*	Trinidad & Tobago	Bahamas	Barbados	Jamaica
39 to 41	select instruments and units of measurement	c	c	c	c	c
	differentiate between the use of centimetres and metres	c	c	c	c	c
	estimate and measure lengths, heights and distances	c	c	c	c	c
	measure perimeters of shapes	c	c	c	c	c
	explain why there is a need for centimetres	c	e	e	e	e
	compare, add and subtract linear measurements	c	c	c	c	c
	develop a sense of kilometres, grams and metres as units of measurement	c	c	c	c	c
	identify real-life situations where kg and g are used	c	c	c	c	c
	estimate, measure, compare and record mass in grams and kilograms	c	c	c	c	c
	compare the masses of different objects	c	c	c	c	c
42	name instruments used to measure temperature	c	e	c	e	c
	work with units used to measure temperature	c	e	c	e	c
	describe recorded temperatures using phrases such as 'warm', 'very hot', etc	c	e	n	e	n
	recognise standard temperature readings such as freezing point, body temperature, and so on	c	e	c	e	c
43	subtract a two-digit number from a three-digit number with or without regrouping	c	c	n	c	n
44 and 45	associate events with specific times	c	e	c	e	e
	use time vocabulary appropriately	c	c	c	c	c
	write the correct notation for times on the hour, half hour, quarter hour	c	c	c	c	c
46 and 47	work with fractions	c	c	c	c	c
48	measure mass	c	c	c	c	c
	collect data through observation, interviews	c	c	c	c	c
	read and interpret information from a bar graph	c	c	c	c	c
	use tally charts, tables and graphs	c	c	c	c	c
49 and 50	calculate the total cost of a set of items	c	c	c	c	c
	subtract a two-digit number from a three-digit number with or without regrouping	c	c	n	c	n
	make amounts of money using various combinations of coins	c	c	c	c	c
	write correct time notations	c	c	c	c	c
	work with fractions	c	c	c	c	c
	solve real-life problems involving mass and height	c	c	n	c	n
51 to 55	identify and name points, lines, rays, angles and right angles	c	e	c	e	c
	identify angles that are equal to, greater than, and smaller than a right angle	c	e	n	n	n
	identify, draw and construct cubes, cuboids, cylinders, cones, spheres	c	c	c	c	c
	count and describe the sides and angles of plane shapes	c	c	c	c	c
	use a ruler to draw and measure lines	c	c	c	c	c
	identify solids in the environment and describe their uses	c	c	c	c	c
	describe differences and similarities between shapes in the environment	c	c	c	c	c
	identify similarities between cubes and cuboids, and between cones and cylinders	c	c	c	c	c
	identify parts of three-dimensional shapes: faces, edges and vertices	c	c	c	c	c
56 to 60	recall basic facts of addition and subtraction	c	c	c	c	c
	add and subtract whole numbers to three digits, with and without regrouping	c	c	c	c	c
	multiply two-digit numbers by one-digit numbers	c	c	c	c	c
	understand multiplication as repeated addition	c	c	c	c	c
	use division to check multiplication answers	c	c	c	c	c
	work with expanded notation	c	c	c	c	c
61	identify shapes and angles	c	c	c	c	c
	use operations to solve word sums	c	c	c	c	c
62 and 63	round off two-digit numbers to the nearest ten	c	c	c	c	c
	use rounding off to estimate for addition and subtraction	c	c	c	c	c
	round off three-digit numbers to the nearest ten	c	c	c	c	c
64 and 65	estimate and measure capacity of containers	c	c	c	c	c
	use litres, millilitres and centilitres for measuring capacity	c	c	c	c	c
	describe real-life uses for measuring capacity	c	c	c	c	c
66 to 68	state and write dates in a variety of ways	c	c	c	c	c
	state the relationship between units of time, including hours and minutes, years and months, weeks and days	c	c	c	c	c
	create and solve problems using time	c	c	c	c	c
69	add and subtract with and without regrouping	c	c	n	c	n
70 and 71	identify and name solid shapes	c	c	c	c	c
	solve word problems involving multiplication	c	c	c	c	c
	compare capacities of different containers	c	c	c	c	c
	round off to the nearest ten	c	c	c	c	c
	work with calendars	c	c	c	c	c
	write dates	c	c	c	c	c
	subtract with regrouping	c	c	c	c	c
72 and 73	use the terms metre and centimetre	c	c	c	c	c
	estimate, measure and compare lengths in metres and centimetres	c	c	c	c	c
	differentiate between kilometres, metres and centimetres	c	c	c	c	c
	collect and record data	c	c	c	c	c
	compare results	c	c	c	c	c
	explain the advantages of representing data in tables and graphs	c	c	c	c	c
	estimate and measure area using square centimetres	c	c	c	c	c
	create and solve problems using linear measurements	c	c	n	n	n

*OECS includes Anguilla, Antigua & Barbuda, British Virgin Islands, Dominica, Grenada, Montserrat, St Kitts & Nevis, St Lucia, St Vincent & the Grenadines

Units	Objectives	OECS*	Trinidad & Tobago	Bahamas	Barbados	Jamaica
74	describe the $5, $10, $20 and $50 notes	c	e	n	c	n
	calculate the total cost of a set of items	c	c	c	c	c
	calculate change	c	c	c	c	c
	approximate to the nearest $1, $10 or $100	c	c	c	c	c
	read and write money amounts to $999.99 using the $ symbol and decimal point	c	c	e	c	c
	round off answers to the nearest $1, $10, $100	c	c	c	c	c
75	multiply by 1 and 0	c	c	c	c	c
76 and 77	read information from pictographs	c	c	n	c	n
	explain why it may be necessary to use one picture or block to represent more than one unit of data	c	c	n	n	n
78 and 79	describe how to collect data using observation and interviewing	c	e	n	n	n
	explain when it is appropriate to use observation and interviews to collect data	c	e	n	n	n
	create problems that may be answered through data collection, representation and interpretation	c	c	n	n	n
	plan for data collection activities	c	c	n	n	n
	collect sets of data through observation and interviews to answer questions of interest	c	c	n	n	n
	select an appropriate method (pictograph or bar graph) and scale to represent a set of collected data	c	c	n	n	n
80	compare linear measurements	c	c	n	c	n
	write numbers as words and use expanded notation	c	c	c	c	c
	multiply by 1 and 0	c	c	c	c	c
81	identify numerator and denominator	c	c	c	c	c
	identify fractions of a group or whole	c	c	c	c	c
	place unit fractions in serial order	c	c	c	c	c
	order fractions with the same numerator	c	c	c	c	c
	use < and > to compare two fractions	c	c	c	c	c
	recognise equivalent fractions	c	c	c	c	c
82 to 86	divide a two-digit number by a one-digit number without remainders	c	c	c	c	c
	use division to find out how many members are in equivalent sets	c	c	c	c	c
	solve division problems, using the correct symbols	c	c	c	c	c
	know and use the relationship between × and ÷ tables	c	c	c	c	c
87 to 92	use several strategies to recall basic facts related to multiplication and division	c	c	n	c	n
	solve problems involving addition of whole numbers, with totals up to 999	c	c	n	c	n
	solve problems involving subtraction of numbers with up to three digits	c	c	n	c	n
	identify odd and even numbers	c	e	c	c	c
	estimate and check addition and subtraction problems	c	e	c	c	c
	work with a number line	c	e	c	c	c
	solve problems involving addition and subtraction in the same problem	c	e	c	c	c
93 and 94	work with litres and half-litres	c	c	c	c	c
	use <, > and = to compare the capacity of groups of containers	c	c	c	c	c
95 and 96	solve addition problems using regrouping	c	c	c	c	c
	add three two-digit numbers	c	c	c	c	c
97	add two proper fractions with like denominators	c	e	n	n	n
	solve problems involving addition of fractions and fractions of a group of objects	c	e	n	n	n
98 to 100	work with litres and half-litres	c	c	c	c	c
	use <, > and = to compare the capacity of groups of containers	c	c	c	c	c
	divide whole numbers, using objects and shapes to help with division	c	c	c	c	c
	differentiate between even and odd numbers	c	c	c	c	c
	add three numbers	c	c	c	c	c
	round off to the nearest ten	c	c	c	c	c
	estimate, measure and compare length	c	c	c	c	c
	read and write prices	c	c	c	c	c
	work out the total cost of a group of similarly priced items	c	c	c	c	c
	work with sets	e	e	c	c	c
	use the vocabulary associated with sets	e	e	c	c	c
	solve word problems involving division	c	c	c	c	c
101 and 102	sort examples of the cube, cuboid, cylinder, cone, and sphere	c	c	n	c	n
	identify the similarities and differences between the cube and cuboid	c	e	n	c	n
	identify the vertices of 3D shapes	c	e	n	c	n
	describe 3D shapes in terms of the number of vertices, and the type of faces	c	e	n	c	n
103 to 107	discover, memorise and recall multiplication facts	c	c	c	c	c
	find unknown factors or products using number lines, arrays and facts	c	c	c	c	c
	explain the commutative property of factors in a multiplication sentence	c	c	c	c	c
	multiply a two-digit number by 10 and 100	c	c	n	n	n
	understand multiplication as repeated addition	c	c	c	c	c
	compare products using < or >	c	c	c	c	c
	use rounded numbers to estimate products	c	c	c	c	c

*OECS includes Anguilla, Antigua & Barbuda, British Virgin Islands, Dominica, Grenada, Montserrat, St Kitts & Nevis, St Lucia, St Vincent & the Grenadines

Units	Objectives	OECS*	Trinidad & Tobago	Bahamas	Barbados	Jamaica
108 to 111	identify plane shapes including squares, circles, triangles, rectangles, (and describe squares, rectangles and triangles in terms of the number and length of their sides) pentagons and hexagons	c	c	c	c	c
	identify and draw lines of symmetry in shapes and objects	c	c	c	e	c
	explain what a line of symmetry is	c	c	c	e	c
	explain the concept of perimeter	c	c	c	c	c
	estimate, measure and calculate perimeter	c	c	c	c	c
112 to 122	work out the total value of a set of coins or notes	c	c	c	c	c
	count change from notes or coins in common use	c	c	c	c	c
	solve money problems	c	c	c	c	c
	represent different amounts of money	c	c	c	c	c
	use vocabulary related to spending	c	c	c	c	c
	define and use vocabulary related to numbers	c	c	c	c	c
	order numbers	c	c	c	c	c
	relate division to multiplication	c	c	c	c	c
	write pairs of multiplication and division facts	c	c	c	c	c
	use multiplication to check the answer to a division sum	c	c	c	c	c
	use operations to solve word sums	c	c	c	c	c
	use repeated subtraction to divide a two-digit number by a one-digit number with and without remainders	c	c	c	c	c
	use several strategies to recall basic multiplication and division facts	c	c	c	c	c
	write story sums and use multiplication or division to solve them	c	c	c	c	c
123 to 125	estimate, calculate and compare perimeters of flat objects	c		c	c	c
	find the total of a group of similarly priced items	c	c	c	c	c
	work out change in cents	c	c	c	c	c
	identify pairs, half-dozens and dozens	c	c	c	c	c
	draw shapes with a given perimeter	c	c	c	c	c
	use vocabulary associated with numbers	c	c	c	c	c
	compare and order three-digit numbers	c	c	c	c	c
	multiply by ten	c	c	c	c	c
	create and solve problems using addition, multiplication, subtraction and division	c	c	c	c	c
126 to 130	recall basic division facts	c	c	c	c	c
	use several strategies to recall basic multiplication and division facts	c	c	c	c	c
	solve division as repeated subtraction and inverse of multiplication	c	c	c	c	c
	use operations to solve problems	c	c	c	c	c
131	read dates off a calendar	c	e	c	c	c
	state the relationship between units of time, including hours and minutes, years and months, weeks and days	c	c	c	c	c
	use a calendar to determine the duration of an event	c	e	n	n	n
132	read and write time notation	c	c	c	c	c
	understand am and pm	c	c	c	c	e
	understand the relationship between units of time such as years, days, weeks	c	c	c	c	c
133 to 135	divide a two-digit number by a single-digit number with or without remainders	c	c	c	c	c
	use the language and symbols associated with dividing, grouping and sharing	c	c	c	c	n
	add and subtract fractions with like denominators	c	c	c	c	c
	name parts of an object using fractions	c	c	c	c	c
136	select appropriate units of measurement	c	c	c	c	c
137 and 138	identify straight line segments	c	n	c	c	e
	draw and label line segments	c	e	c	c	c
	identify curves	c	e	n	n	n
	explain the concepts of 'open curve' and 'closed curve'	c	e	n	n	n
	identify and draw open and closed curves	c	e	n	n	n
139 to 143	use computation strategies for mixed operations	c	c	c	c	c
	select an appropriate strategy (calculator, pencil and paper or mental strategy) to investigate number patterns and relationships	c	c	n	n	n
	identify the pattern in a sequence of numbers	c	c	n	c	n
	estimate and check answers	c	c	c	c	c
	create and solve problems involving money	c	c	c	c	c
144 and 145	add and subtract numbers with up to three digits, with regrouping in two columns/places	c	c	n	c	n
146 to 150	add and subtract, with and without regrouping	c	c	n	c	n
	work with simple fractions	c	c	c	c	c
	work with calendars	c	e	c	c	c
	write numbers up to 999 in words and figures	c	c	c	c	c
	write money amounts using the correct notation	c	c	c	c	c
	identify correct units of measurement for different objects	c	c	c	c	c
	identify the number of faces and edges in three-dimensional objects	c	c	c	c	c
	identify straight lines and curved lines	c	e	n	n	n
	solve real-life problems using basic operations	c	c	c	c	c
	solve practical problems involving division and multiplication	c	c	c	c	c

*OECS includes Anguilla, Antigua & Barbuda, British Virgin Islands, Dominica, Grenada, Montserrat, St Kitts & Nevis, St Lucia, St Vincent & the Grenadines